100 SERMON OUTLINES
from the
NEW TESTAMENT

100 SERMON OUTLINES
from the
NEW TESTAMENT

By

JOHN PHILLIPS

MOODY PRESS
CHICAGO

Third Printing, 1981

ISBN: 0-8024-7817-4

Printed in the United States of America

CONTENTS

INTRODUCTION

If you enjoy the New Testament, here are one hundred outlines valuable for the preacher, the Bible class teacher, and all
those who delight in exploring the Bible and who like to do
so in an organized way.

Outlines are like road maps. They help us see where we
are going and keep us on course as we make our way towards
the desired goal. Good, clear, easily remembered outlines are
of great value both for the preacher in the pulpit and for the
person in the pew. They are the sharp, pointed nails that
clinch the argument. They are the cutting edge on the talk
or sermon. They are the surgeon's scalpel that slices right
through to the bone. They are the burrs that fasten themselves in the mind.

Here are 100 outlines, each with a suitable introductory
paragraph that can be used either for setting the stage or for
illustrating the message. With the shorter outlines additional
illustrative material is given. Some of the outlines are brief,
others detailed, and some are capable of expansion into a
whole series of studies or messages.

1

THE THREE WISE MEN

MATTHEW 2:1-11

Matthew's is the gospel of the King. He traces the Lord's ancestry to David in order to establish the throne rights of Jesus. In keeping with his goal of facing his Jewish readers with the Messiahship of Jesus of Nazareth, Matthew records the visit of these Gentile magi and draws attention to their great question—a question that should have aroused all Jerusalem—"Where is he that is born King of the Jews?"

1. WHAT THEY SOUGHT (2:2)
   a. Their question: They were looking for—
      (1) A Man ("where is he")
      (2) A Monarch ("born King")
      (3) A Messiah ("of the Jews")
   b. Their quest
      (1) Revelation ("we have seen")
      (2) Adoration ("we are come to worship")

2. WHAT THEY THOUGHT (2:1-11)
   a. They substituted reason for revelation (2:1-2)
      (which took them to Jerusalem and Herod)
   b. They substituted revelation for reason (2:10-11)
      (which took them to Bethlehem and Christ)

3. WHAT THEY BROUGHT (2:11)
   a. Gold: a gift for a mighty King
   b. Frankincense: a gift for a ministering Priest
   c. Myrrh: a gift for a martyred Prophet

2

THE LORD'S BAPTISM

MATTHEW 3:13—4:11

In His baptism the Lord Jesus identified Himself with the ruined race He had come to save. He was baptized in the Jordan River, which in the Bible consistently symbolizes death. He was baptized of John's baptism, which was a baptism of repentance. He of course had no need for repentance. His obedience to what He knew to be His Father's will demonstrated that "obedience unto death" which marked out each step of His way. His immersion in the chill waters of Jordan foreshadowed that other baptism at Calvary when He was plunged beneath the icy waters of death itself.

1. THE EXERCISE THAT PRECEDED IT (3:13-15)
   a. A controlling exercise
      (1) His movements (3:13a)
      (2) His motives (3:13b)
   b. A convicting exercise (3:14)
   c. A consistent exercise (3:15)
      (1) Seen in His boyhood: subject to His human father
      (2) Seen in His baptism: subject to His heavenly Father

2. THE EXPERIENCE THAT ACCOMPANIED IT (3:16-17)
   a. The anointing of the Spirit (3:16)
   b. The announcement of the Father (3:17)

3. THE EXPLOIT THAT FOLLOWED IT (4:1-11)
   Victory over—
   a. The lure of the world (4:5-7)
   b. The lust of the flesh (4:1-4)
   c. The lies of the devil (4:8-10)

3

THE SERMON ON THE MOUNT:
The Beatitudes

MATTHEW 5:1-12

The Beatitudes set before us *the victories of the Christ life.*
They demand a philosophy of life, a standard of behavior, a
spiritual resource of divine power. They leave us awed and at
times dismayed, for the Beatitudes demand absolute, undi-
luted perfection. The only person who ever lived the kind of
life envisioned in the Beatitudes and the Sermon on the
Mount is the Lord Jesus Christ. He lived this life openly—
before His family, His friends, His foes, His Father in heaven—
day after day, every moment He drew breath on this planet.
Thus He demonstrated that the principles embodied in the
Beatitudes were not the empty idealism of a dreamer. They
were tested in the red hot crucible of a life that ended at
Calvary.

1. SUBMISSION (5:3)

2. SORROW (5:4)

3. SALVATION (5:5)

4. SATISFACTION (5:6)

5. SYMPATHY (5:7)

6. SANCTIFICATION (5:8)

7. SOUL-WINNING (5:9)

8. SUFFERING (5:10-12)

NOTE: We are not asked to imitate Christ through our own
power. We are told to invite Him into our lives so that He, by
His indwelling Holy Spirit, might live His life in us. That's
the genius of the Christian message. The Christ who gave His
life *for* us also gives His life *to* us. Only He can live the Christian life.

4
THE SERMON ON THE MOUNT: CONTINUED

MATTHEW 5:13—7:27

It stands unique in all the literature of the world. It describes a life-style impossible apart from the regenerating and filling ministries of the Holy Spirit. It is the life of Christ lived out in the life of the believer in a sin-cursed world. It is the Sermon on the Mount. The Beatitudes describe *the victories of the Christ life* (Matt. 5:1-12). The rest of the sermon shows us how to relate the principles of holiness to daily living.

1. THE VITALITY OF THE CHRIST LIFE (5:13-16)
   a. This world is hopelessly corrupt: it needs salt
   b. This world is hopelessly confused: it needs light
2. THE VIRTUE OF THE CHRIST LIFE (5:17-48)
   "But I say unto you." The matter of—
   a. Inconsistency (5:17-20)
   b. Inflammability (5:21-26)
   c. Impurity (5:27-30)
   d. Infidelity (5:31-32)
   e. Integrity (5:33-37)
   f. Injury (5:38-42)
   g. Impartiality (5:43-48)
3. THE VERITIES OF THE CHRIST LIFE (6:1-18)
   "Thy Father which seeth in secret"
   a. Manward—almsgiving (6:1-4)
   b. Godward—praying (6:5-15)
   c. Selfward—fasting (6:16-18)
4. THE VALUES OF THE CHRIST LIFE (6:19—7:27)
   a. False purposes (6:19-34)
   b. False pretences (7:1-5)
   c. False preaching (7:6)
   d. False praying (7:7-11)
   e. False principles (7:12)
   f. False presumptions (7:13-14)
   g. False prophets (7:15-23)
   h. False profession (7:24-27)

THE LORD'S PRAYER

MATTHEW 6:10-13

In his book *The Crisis Of The Christ,* Dr. G. Campbell Morgan points out that there were seven major crises in the life of the Lord Jesus Christ. At each one of these crises the Lord can be seen at prayer. The disciples, impressed by the uniqueness of the Lord's prayer life (so refreshingly different from the stilted, formal, ostentatious, and hypocritical prayer style of the religious leaders of His day), came to Him and said: "Lord, teach us to pray." He did. He taught them the basic principles of prayer in this little gem.

An appreciation of:

1. GOD'S PERSON
   ("Our Father")

2. GOD'S PURPOSES
   ("Thy kingdom come")

3. GOD'S PROVISION
   ("Give us . . . our daily bread")

4. GOD'S PARDON
   ("Forgive us our debts")

5. GOD'S PURITY
   ("Lead us not into temptation")

6. GOD'S PROTECTION
   ("Deliver us from evil")

7. GOD'S POWER
   ("Thine is the kingdom")

JOHN THE BAPTIST'S PROBLEM

MATTHEW 11:3-6

The greatest man born of a woman. That was the Lord's evaluation of His cousin John. Sent before Christ to prepare the way for Him, born to be a priest but preferring the role of a prophet, a preacher of revival whose success was unsurpassed—such was John the Baptist. But now, his revival in ruins, his world reduced to a prison cell, his life only a heartbeat away from Herod's axe, John began to doubt. Had he been mistaken? Was Jesus really the Messiah? With those questions he sent his friends to Jesus to get some straightforward answers, and get them he did!

1. How THE QUESTION WAS ASKED (11:3)
   a. John as a person
      (1) His portentous birth
      (2) His priestly background
   b. John as a preacher
      (1) His was a solitary ministry
      (2) His was a successful ministry
   c. John as a prisoner
      (1) He was expecting death
      (2) He was experiencing doubt

2. How THE QUESTION WAS ANSWERED (11:4-6)
   a. The message Jesus preached
   b. The miracles Jesus performed
      (1) The blind: sin darkens
      (2) The lame: sin disables
      (3) The lepers: sin defiles
      (4) The deaf: sin deafens
      (5) The dead: sin dooms
      (6) The poor: sin despoils
   But Jesus conquers all!

7

THE MYSTERY PARABLES

MATTHEW 13

The Jews had rejected Jesus as Messiah and King. His response was to commence a new form of teaching, one intended to conceal rather than to reveal His meaning. These "mystery" parables of Matthew 13 hid the truth in such a way that only the spiritually enlightened could understand it. They cover the present age when the Kingdom is "underground," so to speak. One day it will be manifested in power; now it is a secret thing. One day the King will come back. In the meantime, His Kingdom must be sought in places, processes, and principles enshrined in these parables.

1. THE EVOLUTION OF CHRISTENDOM
   a. The sower:
      Satan attempting to resist the Kingdom
   b. The wheat and tares:
      Satan attempting to revenge the Kingdom
   c. The mustard seed:
      Satan attempting to rival the Kingdom
   d. The leaven:
      Satan attempting to ruin the Kingdom

2. THE EVALUATION OF CHRISTIANITY
   a. The treasure:
      the value of Christ's cross
   b. The pearl:
      the value of Christ's church
   c. The dragnet:
      the value of Christ's coming

NOTE: The first four parables were spoken beside the sea, to the multitude, the other three indoors to the disciples. The first four thus give the outward manifestation, the last three the inward manifestation.

THE LOAVES AND FISHES

This is the only miracle recorded in all four gospels. It is a delightful study centering in the *lad,* the *loaves,* and the *Lord.* Look at the story through the eyes of the little boy. But don't overlook Andrew. We meet him three times in the gospels. Each time he's leading someone to Christ. Once we see him doing *personal evangelism* with his brother Simon. Once we see him as a *foreign missionary* bringing certain Greeks to Christ. Here we see him doing *children's work.* Note also the basic flaw in both Philip's and Andrew's assessment when Jesus challenged His disciples to feed the multitude. Philip looked at the demand (John 6:7); Andrew looked at the supply (John 6:9). Then both turned and looked at Jesus!

1. THE MESSAGE THE LITTLE BOY HEARD (Luke 9:11)

2. THE MAN THE LITTLE BOY FOLLOWED (John 6:8-9)

3. THE MIRACLE THE LITTLE BOY SAW (John 6:10-12)

4. THE MASTER THE LITTLE BOY TRUSTED (John 6:11)

It is amazing to consider that the Lord Jesus would have gone home hungry that day had not this unnamed little boy been willing to give Him his lunch. Think of it. The Lord of glory, the Creator of heaven and earth, did not have so much as His own crust of bread! And a generous little boy was willing to press into His hands not just one of his little barley loaves, not just a piece of fish, but his whole lunch! This little boy stands in the annals of eternity alongside that widow who cast into the treasury "all her living." Great will be their reward in heaven.

A CAMEO OF THE CHURCH

MATTHEW 16:18; 18:1-35

It is sometimes claimed that the church is not to be found in the gospels. Truth concerning the church is specifically a post-Pentecostal revelation found in the Acts and the epistles, particularly the Pauline epistles. This is generally true. However, on two occasions Christ made prophetic statements about the church. These two references give us, in embryonic form, the very essence of the church as it later unfolded historically in Acts and theologically in the epistles.

1. THE UNIVERSAL CHURCH (16:18)

2. THE LOCAL CHURCH (18:1-35)
   a. The reception of believers (18:1-10)
   b. The restoration of backsliders (18:11-19)
   c. The reconciliation of brethren (18:20-35)

NOTE: The universal church was not founded upon Peter, as the Roman Catholics maintain. It was founded upon Christ. "Thou art *Peter,*" the Lord said. The word is *petros,* a loose, movable stone, a pebble. "Upon this *rock* I will build my church." The word for *rock* is *petra,* signifying a mass of immovable rock. For instance, the modern name for Seir, the ancient rock-hewn stronghold of Edom, is Petra. The church is built upon Christ, not on Peter the pebble. Some maintain that the church is built on Peter's confession. However, Peter's confession brings us directly back to Christ, the Son of the living God.

10

THREE RICH MEN

Mark 10:17-22; Luke 12:16-20; Luke 16:19-31

Wondering if these three rich men were not one and the same person at three stages in his career is a provocative thought! Even though the actual *person* is not the same (Luke 12 records a parable, with fictitious people), the *principle* is the same. Here we have a progression. First the rich young ruler, so attractive, so enthusiastic, so open, yet making the fatal choice concerning Christ. Then the hard-nosed business tycoon with his vast holdings and his selfish, narrow interests. Then the dead and damned man. It is a solemn message.

1. A BURDENED MAN: "Too much!"
   a. His search
      (1) How he came to Jesus
      (2) What he confessed to Jesus
   b. His sorrow

2. A BUSINESS MAN: "Too hard!"
   a. His problem
   b. His proposal
      (1) I will further enrich myself
      (2) I will fairly enjoy myself

3. A BURIED MAN: "Too late!"
   a. His pains—they were real
   b. His prayers—they were refused

11

MARKS OF A HYPOCRITE

MATTHEW 23

The Lord's Beatitudes in Matthew 5 contrast with His woes in Matthew 23. The Pharisees were for the most part, the very embodiment of hypocrisy. The word hypocrite comes to us from a word that means "to act upon the stage." In other words, a hypocrite is an actor, or a pretender. The Pharisees were the great religious pretenders of their day. Jesus strips off their stage mask and, in so doing, exposes hypocrisy in all its forms.

1. WHAT THEY SOUGHT (23:1-12)
   a. The admiration of men (23:1-5)
   b. The advancement of men (23:6)
   c. The adulation of men (23:7-12)

2. WHAT THEY TAUGHT (23:13-22)
   The "woe" against—
   a. Their preaching (23:13)
   b. Their prayers (23:14)
   c. Their proselytes (23:15)
   d. Their principles (23:16-22)

3. WHAT THEY WROUGHT (23:23-28)
   The "woe" against—
   a. Their show of religion (23:23-24)
   b. Their show of respectability (23:25-26)
   c. Their show of righteousness (23:27-28)

4. WHAT THEY THOUGHT (23:29-36)

O JERUSALEM

MATTHEW 23:37-38

What a city it was! It crowned the high hills of Judea like a glorious diadem. It had an unbroken history reaching back to the days of Abraham and Melchizedek. It was the home of the Temple, the spot where the eternal God abode amongst men. It was the citadel of the faith, the sacred depository of the hopes, beliefs, and aspirations of the Hebrew people. Jerusalem! It had been besieged and ravaged, rebuilt and stormed and sacked again more times than men could count. Now it had rejected its rightful King and within a generation would be handed over to the tender mercies of the legions of Rome. Over that city Jesus wept, as perhaps He still weeps over the great, sad cities of this sin-cursed earth.

1. WHAT WEEPING
   "O, Jerusalem!"

2. WHAT WICKEDNESS
   "Thou that killest"

3. WHAT WARMTH
   "How often would I"

4. WHAT WISDOM
   "As a hen"

5. WHAT WILFULNESS
   "Ye would not"

6. WHAT WOE
   "Your house . . . desolate"

HE WENT A LITTLE FARTHER

MATTHEW 26:39

How far He had already come! Out of the ivory palaces, into a world of woe! From the pinnacle of glory to that Bethlehem barn! All the long way from the bosom of the Father to the womb of the virgin. He had been to Bethlehem, to Egypt, to Nazareth, to Capernaum and the lake country, around and about Galilee, north and south, east and west, as a pilgrim preacher, an itinerant prophet, a homeless stranger in the world His hands had made. And now He went a little farther. He went that dark and dreadful "second mile." Trace the steps! Measure their length. Span the great yawning gulf of agony that each step spanned until He came to the last of them all—that giant leap back whence He came.

1. GETHSEMANE
   (Victory over the flesh)

2. GABBATHA
   (Victory over the world)

3. GOLGOTHA
   (Victory over Satan)

4. GRAVE
   (Victory over death and hades)

5. GLORY
   (Victory over time and sense)

THE MAN WHO CRUCIFIED CHRIST

MATTHEW 27:33-54

He was a Roman soldier, a centurion. Beyond that he is a stranger to us. His age, his appearance, his nationality, his personality, his career, his abilities, his family—of these we know nothing at all. He was a soldier charged with the execution of a death sentence in Jerusalem. He is one of the men who actually crucified Christ. His voice, however, rings down through the centuries. In the face of the overwhelming and mounting evidence, in the teeth of Pilate and the priests, he proclaimed his dawning faith. Jesus was the Son of God!

1. CRUCIFYING CHRIST
   He endorsed the world's verdict

2. CONSIDERING CHRIST
   Never before had he seen such—
   a. Personality
   b. Pain
   c. Power (the Calvary miracles)

3. CONFESSING CHRIST
   "This was the Son of God."

NOTE: The Calvary miracles were impressive. There was darkness over all the land. "Give us a sign from heaven," Christ's enemies had demanded. When He was born He put a new star in the sky, when He died He put out the sun. The rocks were rent. When the Pharisees objected to the multitudes' hailing Jesus with their hosannas, He said, "If these should hold their peace, the stones would immediately cry out" (Luke 19:40). And so the rocks did when they were rent. The graves burst open. Most impressive of all, from the Jewish point of view, the Temple veil was rent asunder, signifying the end of Judaism as a meaningful religion. The centurion was awed by these signs.

THE ANNUNCIATION

LUKE 1:31-33

The angel Gabriel brought the tidings to earth. He came down twice: once to see a man, once to see a woman; once to visit a priest, once to visit a peasant; once to call upon a very old man, once to call upon a very young virgin. The man doubted, the woman burst into song. And that song has gone on making music in human hearts ever since. And what raised that song? The annunciation! The news that she, of all the women who had ever lived, was to be the mother of God's eternal Son made flesh. In the annunciation, the angel Gabriel proclaimed both comings of Christ. Mary could not see the wide centuries that divided the two halves of the annunciation. We can.

1. CHRIST'S COMING TO REDEEM (1:31-32)
   a. The importance of that advent (1:31)
      (1) The miracle of it
          ("Thou shalt conceive")
      (2) The meaning of it
          ("Call his name JESUS")
   b. The impact of that advent (1:32a)
      (1) The unparallelled fame to be His
          ("He shall be great")
      (2) The unparallelled claim to be His
          ("Called the Son of the Highest")

2. CHRIST'S COMING TO REIGN (1:32-33)
   a. By divine right (1:32b)
      ("The throne of his father David")
   b. In dynamic might (1:33)
      (1) The center of His Kingdom
          "The house of Jacob"
      (2) The circumference of His Kingdom
          ("of his kingdom . . . no end")

16

THE VIRGIN MARY

There are more than half a billion Roman Catholics in the world, and every devout Roman Catholic is devoted to Mary as the "Mother of God." The center of Mariolatry is in one of the great Roman Catholic churches in Rome itself. In the courtyard of that church is a great, lofty cross. Mary and Jesus are both nailed to that cross, crucified back to back. For to Rome, Mary is just as much our redeemer as Jesus is. The New Testament knows no such Mary.

1. MARY AND THE COMING OF CHRIST
   a. Her confession in connection with His birth
      (1) What she said when the birth was announced (Luke 1:26-38)
      (2) What she did when the birth was accomplished (Luke 2:21-24) (she took her place as a sinner)
   b. Her confusion in connection with His boyhood (Luke 2:41-52)

2. MARY AND THE CAREER OF CHRIST
   a. Her confrontation with Jesus, the Master (John 2:1-12)
   b. Her confrontation with Jesus, the Man (Matt. 12:46)
   c. Her confrontation with Jesus, the Mediator (John 19:25-27) (Jesus sent her away from the scene)

3. MARY AND THE CAUSE OF CHRIST (Acts 1:12-14)
   When last seen in Scripture, she was in the upper room with the disciples, not as the "Mother of God" but as a child of God. She was awaiting with all the others the coming of the Holy Spirit.

17

THE BOY JESUS

LUKE 2:41-52

A visit to the city of Jerusalem! Of all the places in Jerusalem that interested Him, the Temple enthralled Him most. In that Temple area He would assuredly stand, transfixed by the blood-stained altar, watching with troubled eyes the sacrifices and the ascending smoke. Passages from Isaiah and the Psalms would stir His soul. "Brought as a lamb to the slaughter" (Isa. 53:7). "They pierced my hands and my feet" (Ps. 22:16). By this time He knew full well who He was and who His Father was. Yes, and He knew what His Father's business was in this world of sin. Why it took Joseph and Mary three days to find Him will ever remain a mystery. Surely they should have made a beeline to the Temple!

1. THEIR TRAGIC MISTAKE (2:44)

2. THEIR TEARFUL MISSION (2:45-48)

3. THEIR TEMPLE MEETING (2:46)
   a. Their criticism of Him (2:48)
   b. His correction of them
      (1) His sovereignty under God (2:49-50)
      (2) His surrender unto God (2:51-52)

NOTE: A whole day's journey without Christ! How often could such a statement be written across the life of a believer. To get up in the morning, eat a hasty breakfast, hurry off to work or the daily round of activities, to find the evening hours crowded, and to tumble, tired, into bed at night and fall right off to sleep—a whole day without thought or word of Him! A famous concert pianist once said, "If I fail to practice for the full time one day I know it, if I neglect my practice for two days the conductor knows it, if I do not practice for three days everybody knows it." The same principle is true in the Christian life. Let us never again go a whole day's journey without Him.

THE WOMAN WHO LOVED MUCH

LUKE 7:44-47

Who was she? What dark sin stained her soul? Where did she find the courage to come, to dare the Pharisee's scorn? How did she know that Jesus would not be embarrassed, would not chase her away? Did she dare to believe that this Friend of publicans and sinners would read her heart and defend her in the face of hostility and scorn? What a lesson this woman has taught the world of penitence! What a stage she set up that day—a stage upon which the Christ of God could manifest His wisdom, love, and power! It will be one of the joys of heaven to meet this woman and shake her hand and thank her for what she did.

1. HER OUTRIGHT PENITENCE (7:44)
   ("But")

2. HER OUTPOURED PASSION (7:45-46)
   ("But")

3. HER OUTWARD PREPARATION (7:47)
   ("But")

NOTE: The buts of the Bible are always interesting. Like the hinges upon which massive doors swing, so these buts are usually the hinges upon which a story turns. Mark them in the lives of such people as Solomon, Uzziah, the prodigal son. On the three buts in the story here, we trace the forward movement of this woman's growth in grace from *contrition* through *consecration* to *coronation*.

19

THE RICH FOOL

Luke 12:16-20

People said he was a success. God said he was stupid, a fool. That is the force of the word. It means, literally, "a senseless one." Men would point him out to their sons. They would point out his mansion on the hill, his thoroughbred Egyptian horses, his golden coach, his liveried servants. God points him out too and draws attention to his unsaved soul. The man made three mistakes. He measured success in material terms alone. He thought a soul could be satisfied with beef and beer. He thought he was going to live and live and live.

1. He Mistook His Bankbook for His Bible (12:18)

2. He Mistook His Body for His Soul (12:19)

3. He Mistook Time for Eternity (12:19-20)
   ("Many years . . . this night")

Illustration: Imagine a young man presenting his loved one with an engagement ring worth many hundreds of dollars, but it is enclosed in a little box lined with black velvet worth less than a dollar. Picture the girl being captivated by the box and ignoring the diamond. "Oh, what a cute little box. Isn't it pretty? I just adore it. I'll treasure it forever. Wherever did you get it? I think it's just darling." Would we not say that there's something radically wrong with the girl's sense of values? Of course we would! But there are many who are just as foolish, perhaps more foolish, in the relative value they place on their body as compared wth the value they place on their soul.

EXCUSES

LUKE 14:16-24

It is astonishing what excuses people make for not coming to Christ. Some people are too busy to bother; some are too clever to come; some are too religious to repent; some are too worldly to want to; some too proud to pray. The Lord Jesus once focussed on this problem. He told a story in which three kinds of men emerged together with their empty reasons for not responding to the invitation. And with a sure hand He drew the picture of the consequences. They rejected the invitation. Very well, they too would be rejected.

1. THE BUSINESS MAN'S EXCUSE: "My wealth!" (14:18)

2. THE WORKING MAN'S EXCUSE: "My work!" (14:19)

3. THE FAMILY MAN'S EXCUSE: "My wife!" (14:20)

ILLUSTRATION: When Queen Elizabeth II was to be crowned, she sent an invitation to those of her subjects chosen to be present for that occasion. The invitation was sent to peers of the realm, to members of her government, to representatives of the common people. But every invitation bore the same closing statement: "All excuses ceasing." For when royalty issues an invitation it is no ordinary matter. It is a command. Thus the Lord's gospel invitation is a command; making an excuse is nothing short of rebellion.

21

TWO LOST SONS

Luke 15:11-32

There were two boys. Of the two, the wayward prodigal is by far the most likeable, the most attractive, the most honest and open. Both were equally lost—the prodigal amongst the pigs and the other in his pew. The father loved them both.

The context is important. The parable was addressed to two kinds of people, the scribes and Pharisees and the publicans and sinners. The publicans and sinners saw themselves in the prodigal; the scribes and Pharisees, to their rage and scorn, saw themselves in the older brother.

1. THE REBELLIOUS SON
   a. His going-away prayer
      ("Father, give me")
   b. His coming-home prayer
      ("Father, . . . make me")

2. THE RELIGIOUS SON
   a. His actions betrayed him
      ("He was angry, and would not go in")
   b. His argument betrayed him
      ("Thou never gavest me a kid, that I might make merry")
   c. His attitude betrayed him
      ("I," "me," "my")

NOTE: This is really the parable of the Father's heart. The father is mentioned no less than twelve times in the double parallel. It gives us a glimpse of God almost unique in the Bible. God is rarely called "Father" in the Old Testament. Indeed, the incidents in which He is so named can be counted on one hand. Jesus came to teach us a new name for God, the greatest name of all—Father!

HELL IS FOR REAL

LUKE 16:19-31

Jesus spoke more about hell than He did about heaven. Indeed, it was because He knew so well the reality of that dreadful place that He came down here to warn and woo the sons of men. This passage is a statement of fact, not a parable. It records an incident torn from real life. The language may well be figurative, although some, perhaps, would question that, but hell is real. He who said "I am . . . the truth" and who loved men enough to die for them confronts us with this solemn scene.

1. WE DO NOT KNOW WHO THIS MAN WAS:
   There is no record of his name. It is not in the book of life.

2. WE DO KNOW WHERE THIS MAN WENT:
   He went to a place of conscious torment.

3. WE ALSO KNOW WHAT THIS MAN WANTED:
   Too late—
   a. He wanted to pray.
      ("Father Abraham")
   b. He wanted to preach.
      ("I have five brethren")

NOTE: Here are the verses in which Jesus referred to heaven: Matthew 5:12; 6:20; 7:14; 13:33; 19:17, 21; 25:26; Mark 10:21, 30; Luke 6:23; 10:20; 12:33; 16:22, 25; 18:22; John 3:13; 4:14, 36; 5:24, 39; 6:27, 40, 47, 54; 10:28; 12:25; 14:2-3; 17:2-3.

Here are the verses in which He referred to hell: Matthew 5:22, 29-30; 7:13; 8:12; 10:15, 28; 11:22-24; 12:36, 41-42; 13:40, 42, 50; 16:18; 18:8-9; 22:13; Mark 3:29; 9:43, 45, 47; 12:40; Luke 10:14-15; 11:31-32; 12:5; 16:23-25, 28; 20:47; John 5:22, 24, 27, 29-30; 9:39; 12:31; 16:8, 11; 17:12.

23

THE COLT OF AN ASS

LUKE 18:29-36; EXODUS 24:20

Jesus rode in triumph in Jerusalem on the colt of an ass. Why such an animal as this? Why not a war-horse or a stately camel? There are several reasons, of course. One was that His Kingdom was not of this world and He paid scant heed to this world's ideas of pomp. Another reason is suggested by that interesting law recorded in Exodus 24:20. The firstborn son of a man had to be redeemed; so did the firstborn foal of an ass. In both cases a lamb had to be slain. In the case of the colt, if the owner was not prepared to redeem the creature he had to break its neck. Carry that truth over to the story of this colt and it becomes an object lesson to the ages. It symbolizes man in all his need of One who can redeem him and bring his wayward spirit to harness.

The creature needed to be

1. REDEEMED (Exodus 24:20)

2. RELEASED (Luke 18:30)

3. RULED (Luke 18:35)

NOTE: Christ's ability to ride an unbroken colt through wildly cheering and demonstrating crowds is yet another evidence of His deity and His total mastery over all the world of nature. We all know how wildly an unbroken colt will react to being saddled! Not this one! It instantly owned Jesus as its Lord.

THE PARABLE OF THE POUNDS

Luke 19:11-27

The parable of the pounds is not a repetition of the parable of the talents. The parable of talents suggests the surrender of one's gifts and abilities to further the interests of Him who bestowed them. The parable of the pounds suggests the surrender of ourselves. There is a distinct dispensational flavor to this parable. It anticipates the return of the King. All is seen in the light of that. Jesus is coming again to evaluate how we have lived our lives.

1. What the King Explained
   a. His future
   b. His friends
   c. His foes

2. What the King Expected
   a. Personal involvement
   b. Personal investment

3. What the King Exposed
   a. The significance of faithfulness
   b. The seriousness of failure

Note: This parable is told only in Luke's gospel. The incident behind the parable would have been well known to those who first heard it. Herod the Great and his son Archelaus had actually gone from Jericho (where the parable was spoken and where Archelaus had just rebuilt his palace) to Rome to receive the sovereignty. Herod Antipas later did the same thing.

THE MAN CRUCIFIED WITH CHRIST

LUKE 23:32-43; MATTHEW 27:44

At nine o'clock that morning they nailed this man cursing, fighting, screaming to his cross. Not long afterwards they broke his legs and hurled him into eternity. He went straight to paradise. He was not baptised, confirmed, or enrolled in any church. He confessed to no priest although there were plenty standing by. He did no penance. He had no claim to moral character. He did not ask the virgin Mary to pray for him, even though she was present. He called on none of the saints. He was a lost soul on his way to an imminent hell when suddenly, He flung his soul at Jesus' feet. He heard the gospel from Christ's enemies ("He saved others . . .") and he turned in wondrous faith to Jesus. And he was saved, instantly, then and there, on the same grounds and in the same way anyone is saved. And he received immediate assurance of his salvation, too.

1. HE WAS A DYING MAN
   He owned—
   a. The legality of his sentence
   b. The load of his sin

2. HE WAS A DISCERNING MAN
   He began to—
   a. Look at Jesus
   b. Listen to Jesus

3. HE WAS A DELIVERED MAN
   "To day . . . paradise!"

26

THE PLACE CALLED CALVARY

LUKE 23:33

Calvary! The name is familiar to us from a hundred hymns. It is sweetest music in our ears. It tells us of sins forgiven, of peace with God, of life for evermore. But, strange to say, the actual word occurs only once in the Bible (King James Version). "And when they were come to the place, which is called Calvary, there they crucified him." Take those last four words. Emphasize each one in turn. You will have the anatomy of a crime—the darkest, foulest, most monstrous crime ever committed on this sin-cursed planet earth.

1. THE PLACE
There!

2. THE PEOPLE
They!

3. THE PENALTY
Crucified!

4. THE PERSON
Him!

NOTE: Since it was Passover time, Jerusalem would have been crowded with Jewish visitors from scores of lands. It has been estimated that something like a million people would have been present. Acts 2:8-11 gives us a roll call of the various nations still represented in the city a couple of months later at Pentecost. The crucifixion of Christ, then, took place before the eyes of the world.

THE WORD WAS MADE FLESH

JOHN 1:1-4, 14

As a thought must be clothed in words before it can be known, so God needed to clothe Himself in flesh. John's mystical statement declares beyond question the absolute, eternal deity of the Lord Jesus as well as the manner and the meaning of His entry into human life.

1. THE INFINITE CREATOR (1:1-3)
   a. His unique person (1:1)
      (1) He is eternally God
          ("In the beginning was the Word")
      (2) He is equally God
          ("And the Word was with God")
      (3) He is essentially God
          ("And the Word was God")
   b. His universal power (1:2-3)

2. THE INCARNATE CREATOR (1:14)
   a. His translation to humanity
   b. His transformation of humanity

NOTE: John's gospel is the gospel of Jesus as the Son of God, with special emphasis on His absolute deity. That is why John does not tell us about the birth in Bethlehem or any of the associate events. The closest he gets to the cradle is in 1:14 and 3:16. In Matthew and Luke the Lord Jesus is the "child . . . born" of Isaiah's prophecy (Isa. 9:6) ; in John He is the "son . . . given."

YE MUST BE BORN AGAIN

JOHN 1:11-13; 3:1-10

A woman once asked the great preacher George Whitefield why he so often preached from the text "Ye must be born again." "Madam," he said, "because ye *must* be born again!" It is a grand gospel theme. The story in John 3 gives us the fact; the statement in John 1 gives us the formula. Taken together they make the mystery plain.

1. THE NEWS OF THE NEW BIRTH
   Nicodemus was lost even though he was—
   a. Politically, a member of the Sanhedrin
   b. Socially, a master in Israel
   c. Religiously, a model Pharisee

2. THE NEED FOR THE NEW BIRTH
   "Ye must be born again." "That which is born of the flesh is flesh."

3. THE NATURE OF THE NEW BIRTH
   a. Three negatives
      (1) Not of human descent
          ("Not of blood")
      (2) Not of human desire
          ("Not . . . of the will of the flesh")
      (3) Not of human design
          ("Not . . . of the will of man")
   b. Three positives
      (1) Man must believe on His name (Jesus—"Saviour")
      (2) Man must receive
      (3) God works the regenerating miracle ("Become!")

A LESSON IN OBEDIENCE

JOHN 2:5

The Roman Catholic Church teaches that we should pray to the virgin Mary and that often prayers to her are more effective than prayers to Christ. The reasoning behind the dogma is both human and false. "The Lord is often angry with us sinners because of our sins," says Rome. "We dare not come to Him, but we can come to His mother. She will pray for us. She will intercede for us with her Son. He will not deny her prayers." Every time a Roman Catholic recites his rosary he perpetuates the error. Only once in the Bible is a specific request of Mary addressed to the Lord. Instantly the Lord put her in her place. Rebuked, she turned to those who had approached her and directed them to her Son. They were to approach Him with no mediatrix in between.

1. THE CALL TO PERFECT OBEDIENCE
   a. No mental reservations
      ("*Whatsoever* he saith unto you")
   b. No heart rivals
      ("Whatsoever *he* saith unto you")

2. THE CALL TO PERSONAL OBEDIENCE
   ("Whatsoever he saith unto *you*")

3. THE CALL TO PURPOSEFUL OBEDIENCE
   ("Do it")

NOTE: The Protestant Reformation was fought out with Rome over a single word—*only*. Rome will agree that the Lord Jesus is a Priest, but not that Jesus is our only priest; Rome will agree that salvation is by faith, but not that salvation is only by faith; Rome will agree that Jesus is our Mediator, but not that Jesus is our only mediator; Rome will agree that we must confess our sins to God, but not that we must confess them to God only.

EVERYBODY'S TEXT

JOHN 3:16

F. W. Boreham has written an interesting series of volumes on the texts that have made history. He gives us Sir Isaac Newton's text and John Newton's text; Livingstone's text and Luther's text; the text that transformed Cowper and the text that motivated Carey. In each case he shows how a particular text of Scripture molded and made a sinner into a saint. When he comes to John 3:16, he calls it "Everybody's Text." And that's exactly what it is.

1. A REVELATION OF THE HEART OF GOD
   ("For God so loved . . . he gave")

2. A REVELATION OF THE MIND OF GOD
   a. Regarding His Son
   b. Regarding His salvation
      ("Whosoever believeth")

3. A REVELATION OF THE WILL OF GOD
   ("Should not perish, but have")

NOTE: It is probably an accident of translation that in the King James Version of the Bible John 3:16 has exactly twenty-five words. The very center word is the word "Son." Thus all the truth of the text finds its center in Him. The words and thoughts either march resolutely towards Him or radiate majestically from Him. However this fact of translation came about it perfectly illustrates the position God has given to His Son. He is the center of everything. God has no plans, no purposes for men which do not center in the person of His Son.

THE WOMAN AT THE WELL

JOHN 4:3-39

The story illustrates the growth of a soul in the knowledge of Christ. Look at the names the woman uses in referring to the Saviour. "Jew!" she says (v. 9), and one can almost see the sneer on her lips. "Sir," she says (v. 11) with a new respect dawning in her darkened heart. "Prophet!" she exclaims (v. 19) as His words begin to pierce the armor of her soul. "Messias!" she says tentatively (v. 25), the light beginning to break through. "Christ!" she cries triumphantly at last (v. 29) as she gives her testimony back at home.

1. How THE LORD CHOSE HER (4:3-6)
   ("Must needs go through Samaria")

2. How THE LORD CHALLENGED HER (4:7-27)

3. How THE LORD CHANGED HER (4:28-39)

NOTE: "He must needs go through Samaria," we read. It was a divine imperative. Just as we must be born again, just as we must appear before the judgment seat of Christ, so He must needs go through Samaria. It was not a geographical imperative. Indeed, the Jews went miles out of their way in great journeys not to go through Samaria, so great was their hatred of the Samaritans. But He must. For He ever walked in paths ordained of God.

NEW LIFE IN CHRIST

JOHN 11:25-26

Jesus raised three people from the dead. There was a child of twelve sunny summers, only recently deceased, a young man on his way to the graveyard, and a man dead and buried four days and already decomposing in his tomb. D. L. Moody once searched for a text used by Jesus at a funeral. He thought such a text would bring great consolation at the funeral he had to take. He was delighted to discover that Jesus broke up every funeral He ever attended! Here in John 11:25-26 we come as close as we ever shall to one of the Lord's funeral texts. It reveals the three kinds of life Jesus bestows.

1. RESURRECTION LIFE
   ("I am the resurrection, and the life")

2. SPIRITUAL LIFE
   ("He that believeth in me, though he were dead, yet shall he live")

3. ETERNAL LIFE
   ("And whosoever liveth and believeth in me shall never die")

NOTE: Life is a mysterious and complex thing. True, we can now make artificial protein in the laboratory and protein is the building block of life. But it is doubtful if man will ever be able actually to create life, still less to make it out of nothing. To say that life is only chemistry, as some atheistic biochemists do, is grossly to understate the fantastic complexity of even the "simplest" form of life. But Jesus offers life in three dimensions. That we should live again is no more wonderful, after all, than that we should live at all.

SUPPER AT BETHANY

JOHN 12:1-11

What an astonishing meal that must have been! Jews from all over were thronging the street outside, jostling each other in hope of catching a glimpse of a resurrected man. Inside, Lazarus, we are told, "sat at the table with him." But surely that was the table of Lazarus? Yes, but Lazarus had made Jesus Head of his home so he sat at meat with Him. Martha, busy as ever, bustled away in the kitchen, her old spirit of criticism gone. And Mary, as always (compare Luke 10:39 and John 11:32), was at the Master's feet. The focus of the story, of course, comes to rest on Mary's gift and worship.

1. LAZARUS WITNESSING (12:2*b*, 9-11)

2. MARTHA WORKING (12:2*a*)

3. MARY WORSHIPPING (12:3-8)
   How her devotion to Jesus was—
   a. Revealed (12:3)
   b. Rebuked (12:4-6)
   c. Rewarded (12:7-8)

NOTE: The rich man in the torments of a lost eternity (Luke 16) pleaded that Lazarus, the beggar who once had camped at his gate and who now enjoyed eternal bliss, be sent back to earth as a testimony to his brothers. Abraham told him that even if one rose from the dead they would not believe if they would not accept the testimony of the written Word. The next man Jesus raised from the dead was a man named *Lazarus*—and look what they tried to do to him (John 12:10-11).

JESUS, THE WAY

JOHN 14:6

Thomas must have been daydreaming! Jesus had just told them He was going to heaven. Then Thomas caught the tail end of a paragraph. "Whither I go ye know, and the way ye know." He woke up with a start. "We don't know where you're going," he blurted out, "How can we know the way?" In answer, the Lord Jesus gave us one of His very greatest gospel texts.

He is the WAY! That's for *lost* people. He is the TRUTH! That's for *learned* people. For, as we can so clearly see today, divorce social truth from Christ and the result will be Communism; divorce scientific truth from Christ and the result will be conflict; divorce scriptural truth from Christ and the result will be a cult. He is the LIFE! That's for *longing* people.

Jesus answers the questions—

1. How CAN I BE SAVED?
   ("I am the way")

2. How CAN I BE SURE?
   ("I am . . . the truth")

3. How CAN I BE SATISFIED?
   ("I am . . . the life")

ILLUSTRATION: In the grounds of Hampton Court Palace there is a maze built of hedges. In the middle of the maze is a seat where those who are tired of finding their way back out can rest and think things over. There is also a bell there. By ringing the bell the lost person can summon aid. A man will appear, a man who knows the way. Follow him and soon the perplexing paths will resolve into an orderly way. The solution lies in the man!

35

WHAT SHALL I DO WITH JESUS?

JOHN 18:28; MATTHEW 27:22

Pilate's unhappy face peers out at us from each of the four gospels. We see how despite himself, he was forced to face eternal issues and make a personal decision regarding Jesus Christ. He had a good general knowledge of the facts. We can be sure that nothing that happened in the provinces was not reported in the palace. There came a time in his life, however, when he was forced to make a personal investigation into Christ's claims. This led him to his own personal crisis as expressed in his desperate question: "What shall I do then with Jesus which is called Christ?" The answer he received from the crowd was no help.

1. How PILATE FEARED THE CLAIMS OF CHRIST
   Jesus confronted him—
   a. In his personal life
      (The holiness of Jesus exposed his own wickedness)
   b. In his private life
      (His own wife had been confronted by Christ)
   c. In his public life
      (Christ or Caesar?)
2. How PILATE FOUGHT THE CLAIMS OF CHRIST
   He tried to—
   a. Disclaim the issue
      ("You take Him and decide")
   b. Dismiss the issue
      (He sent Him to Herod)
   c. Discuss the issue
      (Jesus had nothing to say to him)
   d. Distract the issue
      ("Jesus or Barabbas?")
   e. Disown the issue
      (He sought refuge in a rite; he washed his hands)
3. How PILATE FACED THE CLAIMS OF CHRIST
   He crucified Him

A CALL TO CONSECRATION

JOHN 21

This scene was intended as a challenge to all the disciples, but it was especially staged by Jesus to get hold of Peter. Peter was tired of waiting. He was going back to business. But those who have put their hand to the gospel plough find themselves spoiled, as a rule, for mere business. The sacred calling is so much higher and holier than the secular. Thus the Lord meets Peter and gives him a fresh commission, one from which he never turned back.

1. HOW THE LORD RECALLED PETER'S FAILURE
   a. The miraculous catch of fish
   b. The fire of charcoal
   c. The three denials
   d. The vain boast
   e. The use of the old name, Simon
      (See Matthew 16:15-17; John 1:42)

2. HOW THE LORD REKINDLED PETER'S FERVOR
   a. "Lovest thou me?" (agape)
      "I love thee" (phileo)
   b. "Lovest thou me?" (agape)
      "I love thee" (phileo)
   c. "Lovest thou me?" (phileo)
      "I love thee" (phileo)

3. HOW THE LORD RESHAPED PETER'S FUTURE
   a. The privilege of shepherding
   b. The price of shepherding
   c. The principle of shepherding

37

WORLD EVANGELISM

ACTS 1:8

"The uttermost part of the earth"! These were the very last words to fall from the lips of Jesus as He left earth for glory. They embody His heartbeat for lost mankind. In this final statement of His will, He left to the disciples His own program for reaching a lost world. The early church in Acts followed the blueprint to the letter and turned the world upside down. The master plan is still in force and no amount of gimmickry or hoopla can improve upon it.

1. THE DISCIPLES NEEDED ENLISTMENT
    The Lord made *His passion* known to them
    ("The uttermost part of the earth")

2. THE DISCIPLES NEEDED ENCOURAGEMENT
    The Lord made *His presence* known to them
    He convinced them of—
    a. The reality of His resurrection (1:3)
    b. The reality of His rapture (1:9)
    c. The reality of His return (1:11)

3. THE DISCIPLES NEEDED ENLIGHTENMENT
    The Lord made *His plan* known to them
    a. It began with the community
        (Jerusalem)
    b. It moved to the country
        (Judea)
    c. It reached to the continent
        (Samaria)

4. THE DISCIPLES NEEDED ENABLEMENT
    The Lord made *His power* known to them
    ("Ye shall receive power . . . the Holy Ghost")

THE CHURCH IN TRANSITION

Acts 2-3; 1 Corinthians 12-14

The period covered by the book of Acts was unique. It marked the period when God set aside Judaism, with its entrenched and privileged status, and introduced the church. It was marked by a period of rapid expansion in church affairs from Jerusalem to Rome. It marked the unique period during which the New Testament was being written, a period when men needed special signs and gifts to tide them over until God's Word had been fully given. Thus, of course, Acts is essentially a history book. We do not go to Acts for our doctrine, we go to the epistles for that. Yet the epistles grew out of the events recorded in Acts. To see the church in transition will help us keep both our perspectives and our principles right.

1. THE PERIOD
   a. There was no written New Testament
   b. The Temple was still standing
   c. The apostles still lived and ministered

2. THE PROBLEMS
   a. There was the Jewish problem
      (The Jews thought they had special status in the church, as they had once had in the world.)
   b. There was the Gentile problem
      (Gentiles began to outnumber Jews. They had special problems with such things as meats and morality.)

3. THE PROVISIONS
   a. There were special sign-gifts
      (Miracles, tongues)
   b. There were special spiritual gifts
      (Apostles, prophets)

TELL ME THE STORY OF JESUS

ACTS 2:22-24

"What think ye of Christ?" (Matt. 22:42). The Lord Himself threw down the challenge. Upon the answer to that question our whole eternity depends. In Him deity and humanity met and merged. In Him God stepped down off His throne and entered the arena of human affairs to deal forever with the age-old mystery of iniquity. We cannot review too often the person and work of Jesus.

1. HIS VIRGIN BIRTH
   a. The miracle of it
   b. The meaning of it

2. HIS VIRTUOUS LIFE
   a. His triumphs over sin
   b. His triumph over Satan
   c. His triumph over situations

3. HIS VICARIOUS DEATH
   a. The foreviews of the cross
      (the Old Testament prophets and Christ's own prophecies)
   b. The facts of the crucifixion
      (the gospels)
   c. The feelings of the Christ
      (the Psalms, especially Psalm 22)

4. HIS VICTORIOUS RESURRECTION
   a. Up from the tomb
   b. Up to the throne

5. HIS VISIBLE RETURN
   a. Coming for us at the rapture
   b. Coming with us at the return

THE EARLY CHURCH IN ACTION

ACTS 2:38-47

The church was born in power on the day of Pentecost. One moment there was no church; the next, there it was. The church will leave the planet the way it came, suddenly, supernaturally. The church is a projection into time of something planned in the heart of God in eternity past. No period of the church's sojourn on this planet is more full of interest than the period that saw it born. Here in Acts 2 we have the first Christian congregation. It is held before us as a cameo of what church congregations should always be like.

We see a group of believers—

1. SAVED BY FAITH (2:38-41a)

2. SEPARATED BY BAPTISM (2:41b)

3. SOUND IN DOCTRINE (2:42a)

4. STRONG IN FELLOWSHIP (2:42b)

5. SIMPLE IN WORSHIP (2:42c)

6. STEDFAST IN PRAYER (2:42d)

7. SANCTIFIED IN LIFE (2:43)

8. SOLD ON THE GOSPEL (2:44-45)

9. SINGING FROM THE HEART (2:46-47a)

10. SUCCESSFUL IN WITNESS (2:47b)

NOTE: The early church had no great cathedrals in which to meet, no elaborate service, no ritual, no rigid liturgies, very little organization, no seminaries, hardly any New Testament Scriptures. But it had power. It had the power of an ungrieved Holy Spirit in its midst, and in less than thirty years it spread itself all over the civilized world in the face of entrenched dislike and growing hatred and scorn.

THE TRIAL AND MARTYRDOM
OF STEPHEN

Acts 6:1—7:60

Jesus stood up to welcome the first church martyr home to heaven. It is, perhaps, no accident that in the Greek language of the New Testament the same word means both "martyr" and "witness." In Stephen both concepts are forever enshrined. His defence before the Sanhedrin reveals his raw courage. As a result of his ringing testimony and triumphant death an arrow of conviction pierced the soul of Saul, an arrow that rankled until the moment of his own conversion on the Damascus road.

1. FILLED WITH THE HOLY SPIRIT TO SERVE (6:1-8)
   a. He was a good man (6:3)
   b. He was a godly man (6:3)
   c. He was a gifted man (6:3, 8)

2. FILLED WITH THE HOLY SPIRIT TO SPEAK (6:7—7:56)
   a. Debating truth (6:9-15)
   b. Defending truth (7:1-50)
      (1) The tremendous heritage of the Jews (7:1-8)
      (2) The traditional hardness of the Jews (7:9-35)
      (3) The tragic history of the Jews (7:42)
      (4) The trivial horizon of the Jews (7:47-50)
   c. Declaring the truth (7:51-54)

3. FILLED WITH THE HOLY SPIRIT TO SUFFER (7:55-60)
   a. He suffered voluntarily (7:55-56)
   b. He suffered victoriously (7:57-60)

THE CONVERSION OF SAUL OF TARSUS

ACTS 9

Saul was born a Jew, was educated a Greek, and was by right a Roman. He was thus a representative man of his age. He understood and appreciated Jewish light, Greek learning, and Roman law. The three worlds of his day, the worlds of religion, culture, and government as represented, respectively, by the Hebrew, the Greek, and the Roman, were native to his soul. He was as much at home in Athens as he was in Rome or Jerusalem. The conversion of Saul of Tarsus was probably the greatest single event in the history of the church after Pentecost. The Lord Jesus Himself came down from heaven to effect the conviction, conversion, and consecration of this chosen vessel.

1. THE MIRACLE OF SAUL'S CONVERSION (9:1-3)
   a. His rugged personality
   b. His religious persuasion
   c. His raging passion

2. THE MANNER OF SAUL'S CONVERSION (9:4-6)
   a. The tremendous revelation to him (9:4)
   b. The total revolution within him (9:5)
   c. The typical resolution by him (9:6)

3. THE MEANING OF SAUL'S CONVERSION (9:15)
   ("a chosen vessel")
   a. God's chosen pioneer
   b. God's chosen penman

TITLES OF GOD'S SON

Acts 16:31

The full name by which we normally address our Saviour is Lord Jesus Christ. These names are full of significance. Not by accident was He called "Jesus," for instance. The name comes to us from the Greek form of the Hebrew name "Joshua." It means "Jehovah the Saviour." It was given to Him because He would "save his people from their sins" (Matt. 1:21). The Holy Spirit uses the three names with discrimination and always in their proper order, depending on the thought to be emphasized.

1. "LORD": THE HEAVENLY TITLE
   He is the Supreme One

2. "JESUS": THE HUMAN TITLE
   He is the Saving One

3. "CHRIST": THE HEBREW TITLE
   He is the Sufficient One
   a. Sufficient as Prophet
   b. Sufficient as Priest
   c. Sufficient as King

NOTE: There is a growing tendency today to address the Lord as "Jesus." It is a sobering fact that, in the gospels, the only ones of whom it is recorded that they so addressed Him are the demons. And He instantly silenced them when they did so. To His disciples He said: "Ye call me Master and Lord: and ye say well; for so I am" (John 13:13). Respect and deepest reverence are due to Him. Note the distance the disciples felt between Him and them after His resurrection. It is a point worth pondering.

MUCH MORE

ROMANS 5:9-20

It was the law of the trespass offering in Old Testament times that the guilty party must get right with the person he had wronged before he could get right with God. But there was more to it than simply saying "I'm sorry" and making full restitution. He had to add twenty percent. Thus the injured party became the gainer. The trespass offering of Christ's amazing sacrifice is what is before us in this phrase "much more." Because of Calvary both God and man have gained. God has gained because He has been able to demonstrate His love amply. Man has gained because he can become heir to sonship with God and an eternal salvation.

1. THE GOVERNMENT OF GOD (5:9)

2. THE GOODNESS OF GOD (5:10)

3. THE GIFT OF GOD (5:15)

4. THE GLORY OF GOD (5:17)

5. THE GRACE OF GOD (5:20)

NOTE: God is a God of the superlative. He always deals with us generously. It is in His very nature to be lavish with His people. "Good measure, pressed down, and shaken together, and running over" (Luke 6:38). That's the way He gives. He does for us not just what we ask—not even what we ask or think. He does "exceeding abundantly above" all we can ask or think (Eph. 3:20)! Count the superlatives in that! This is what lies behind the "much mores" of Romans 5.

THE GRAND TOUR: PHASE 1

ROMANS 5

Romans 5-8 throbs with vital truth for living the Christian life. In these chapters Paul takes us on a grand tour of the enormous vistas and the immense potentials we have in Christ. Each stepping-stone along the way needs to be thoroughly explored. Romans 5 summarizes the great theme of *salvation*; Romans 6-8 sets forth the truths of *sanctification*.

1. THE AUDIENCE CHAMBER (5:1-2)

2. THE WORK ROOM (5:3-5)

3. THE CONDEMNED CELL (5:6-9)

4. THE POWER HOUSE (5:10-11)

5. THE TIME MACHINE (5:12-14)

6. THE GIFT STORE (5:15-19)

7. THE CHARM SCHOOL (5:20-21)

NOTE: Romans 5 is where God finally confronts the evolutionist. There is no room in true biblical 'theology for the notion that man is descended from the beasts and that he has a common ancestor with the larger primates. We might be able to toy with the ideas in Genesis 1, but only at the cost of considerable hedging with the revealed facts. But when we come to Romans 5 it is either evolution or salvation. For God categorically states that the doctrine of salvation hinges on the fact that "by one man sin entered into the world, and death by sin." Two men divide the human family—Adam and Christ; Adam, the federal head of ruined man, and Christ, the Federal Head of redeemed man.

THE GRAND TOUR: PHASE 2

ROMANS 6-8

In these chapters Paul ascends the eternal heights. They are prefaced by the phrase "Jesus Christ our Lord" and they end with the phrase "Christ Jesus our Lord" (5:21; 8:39). For there is the ultimate secret of the victorious Christian life. It is a life in which all horizons are bounded by the Lordship of Jesus Christ.

1. ROMANS 6
    1. The local church (1-4)
    2. The flower garden (5)
    3. The execution hill (6-7)
    4. The burial vault (8-11)
    5. The coronation room (12-14)
    6. The personnel office (15-22)
    7. The accounting department (23)

2. ROMANS 7
    1. The marriage bureau (1-6)
    2. The law court (7-13)
    3. The slave market (14-25)

3. ROMANS 8
    1. The supreme court (1-4)
    2. The school room (5-7)
    3. The battle field (8-9)
    4. The empty tomb (10-13)
    5. The family circle (14-17)
    6. The millennial Kingdom (18-26)
    7. The prayer meeting (25-27)
    8. The eternal ages (28-30)
    9. The treasure chamber (31-34)
    10. The hostile world (35-39)

47

SANCTIFICATION

ROMANS 6

In Romans 6 Paul deals with the *principles* for holy living. In Romans 7 he examines the *problems* of holy living. In Romans 8 he sets forth the *practice* of holy living. Every believer still has with him the old nature, the Adamic nature with which he was born. But he also has the divine nature, the new nature, the nature brought into the life by the Holy Spirit. The old nature, being Adamic, can do nothing right; the new nature, being divine, can do nothing wrong. Since these two natures are perpetually at war, it is imperative that we learn God's plan for practical sanctification.

1. THE BELIEVER'S DEATH WITH CHRIST (6:1-15)
   a. Explained by Paul (6:1-7)
      (a) His biographical illustration (6:1-4)
      (b) His biological illustration (6:5-7)
   b. Experienced by all (6:8-13)
      (a) Comprehending the truth—"know" (6:8-10)
      (b) Counting on the truth—"reckon" (6:11-12)
      (c) Capitulating to the truth—"yield" (6:13)

2. THE BELIEVER'S DOCTRINE OF CHRIST (6:16-18)
   a. Jesus as Lord (6:16)
   b. Jesus as Liberator (6:17-18)

3. THE BELIEVER'S DUTY TO CHRIST (6:19-23)
   a. The binding fetters of the past—now broken! (6:19-20)
   b. The bitter fruits of the past—now blessed! (6:21-22)
   c. The black future of the past—now bright! (6:23)

THE BELIEVER'S OLD NATURE

ROMANS 6:1–7:6

The cross of Christ is God's instrument for delivering us from the old nature. God does not take us back to Pentecost but back to Calvary. He does not give us thrills and chills and some kind of ecstatic experience; He takes us to the cross. It is in our death, burial, and resurrection with Christ that deliverance comes. Jesus died not only *for* me but *as* me! At Calvary, God dealt not only with the question of *sin* and *Satan* but with the question of *self* as well.

The old nature in the believer is likened to—

1. AN OLD MAN (6:6)
   The old man is *now dead*

2. AN OLD MONARCH (6:12-14)
   The old monarch is *now defeated*

3. AN OLD MASTER (6:16-18)
   The old master is *now deposed*

4. AN OLD MARRIAGE (7:1-6)
   The old marriage is *now dissolved*

ILLUSTRATION: An Irishman found a turtle in his back yard. It had been completely decapitated. Its head lay off by itself yet the turtle was still running around, all over the yard. Patrick was amazed and he called his friend Mike over to see it. "It's dead," he said, "but it's still running around." "It can't be dead," said Mike, "or else it would be still." "It is dead," said Patrick; "here's its head and there's its body." The argument grew hotter when along came O'Brian. They decided his verdict should be final. He looked at the turtle and its decapitated head. "It's dead," he decided, "But it don't believe it!" Which is exactly the problem with so many of us.

49

FREE FROM THE LAW

There are three men in Romans 7. There are the *spiritual man* (vv. 1-6), the *natural man* (vv. 7-13), and the *carnal man* (vv. 14-25). In this chapter Paul wrestles with the persistent problem of the flesh. The principles of deliverance he understands. But how to make it work, that's the problem! For the flesh still seems very much alive even though God counts it crucified. He goes back in thought, in this chapter, to his unconverted days. (In verses 7-13 the verbs are all in the past tense.) He draws a striking parallel between his behavior as a *doomed sinner* and his behavior as a *defeated saint*. Note Paul's "four spiritual laws."

1. PAUL AS A DOOMED SINNER—Condemned by Law (7:7-13)
   a. The Law reveals sin (7:7)
   b. The Law revives sin (7:8-9)
   c. The Law reproves sin (7:10-13)

2. PAUL AS A DEFEATED SAINT—Conquered by lust (7:14-25)
   a. How he was fettered (7:14-25a)
      (1) Two great opposing forces that operate *outside* (7:14-21)
         (a) The Law of Sinai (7:14, 16)
         (b) The law of sin (7:14, 21)
      (2) Two great opposing forces that operate *inside* (7:22-25a)
         (a) The law of my mind (7:22-23, 25a)
         (b) The law of my members (7:23, 25a)
   b. How he was freed (7:25b)

THE GOSPEL AND THE JEW

ROMANS 9-11

What about the Jew? The Jew had rejected Christ and had resisted the Holy Spirit. Both the Hebraist Jews of the homeland and the Hellenist Jews of the Dispersion had, nationally, been adamant in rejecting Christ and the gospel. So, what of God's great promises to Israel? Where does the Jew fit in God's plan today? Is there any future for the nation of Israel? Has God cancelled forever or simply postponed the great promises He once made? Paul confronts these questions squarely in these chapters.

1. GOD'S PAST DEALINGS WITH ISRAEL (Rom. 9)
   (key: His sovereignty)

2. GOD'S PRESENT DEALINGS WITH ISRAEL (Rom. 10)
   (key: His salvation)

3. GOD'S PROMISED DEALINGS WITH ISRAEL (Rom. 11)
   (key: His sincerity)

NOTE: In Romans 9 Paul shows that, as a nation, Israel, was persistently rebellious and that only a small remnant constituted the true Israel. In Romans 10 he shows that the Jew today is on the same footing as the Gentile and needs to accept Christ as his Saviour. In Romans 11 he shows that, in a coming day, God will regather and restore Israel and fulfill all the ancient promises, which are centered in the people and the land. The rebirth of the state of Israel is a harbinger of this coming national and spiritual future for Israel once God's purposes in the church are complete.

CHRIST IS ALIVE

ROMANS 10:9

One day Jesus of Nazareth hung on a cross, friendless, forsaken, and alone. It was a death of ignominy and shame, a cruel and violent death, a death reserved for rebels, slaves, and criminals. A few days later He was worshipped enthusiastically by thousands as the Son of God. Something must have happened in between. It did! He rose from the dead. When He hung on the cross He was alone; within fifty years there was a church to His worship in every major city in the Roman Empire.

One day the disciples were huddled in fear for their lives in an upper room with doors and windows barred. A while later they were out on the streets, loudly proclaiming that Jesus was God and defying all the opposition organized government and religion could bring to bear. Something must have happened in between. It did. Jesus rose from the dead.

"God hath raised him from the dead!" It is the greatest news the world has ever heard.

1. THE BASIC ASSUMPTIONS OF THE GOSPEL
   "God hath raised him from the dead."
   a. A proven truth
   b. A personal trust
      "Believe in thine heart"
   c. A public testimony
      "Confess with thy mouth"

2. THE BLESSED ASSURANCE OF THE GOSPEL
   "Thou shalt be saved"

THE ESSENCE OF THE GOSPEL

ROMANS 10:13

This verse reduces the gospel to its simplest possible terms. It reduces it to a call. Anyone can call. A little child can call. Simon Peter illustrates what is needed. He had walked on the waves towards Christ, marvelling at it all. Suddenly he began to sink. "Lord, save me!" he cried. That was all. No logical niceties, no suave philosophical arguments, no inner debates—just a desperate, meaningful call.

1. THE SUBSTANCE OF THE GOSPEL:
   "Shall be saved!"
   a. From the penalty of sin
   b. From the power of sin
   c. From the presence of sin

2. THE SCOPE OF THE GOSPEL:
   "Whosoever!"

3. THE SIMPLICITY OF THE GOSPEL:
   "Call!"

ILLUSTRATION: Salvation is centered in the name of the Lord. What's in a name? Suppose I were to write you out a check for $50,000. It would do you little good! The check would bounce all over North America, because my name is not good for that kind of money. But suppose one of the Rockfellers were to write you out a check for that amount. It would be a different story. The check might be drawn on the same bank, dated the same day, typed on the same typewriter. The only difference is in the name. It is no use bringing to God the name of the virgin Mary, or the name of Muhammad or Buddha. These are bankrupt names. God only honors, for salvation, the name of His Son.

THE JUDGMENT SEAT OF CHRIST

ROMANS 14:12; 1 CORINTHIANS 3:12-15;
2 CORINTHIANS 5:10-11; REVELATION 3:11

The judgment seat of Christ is for believers. It must not be confused with the great white throne judgment, which is for the unsaved. The believer's sins have all been dealt with at the cross. At the judgment seat, however, he will give account of the way he spent his life as a believer.

1. THE PLAN
   "We must all appear." "Every one . . . shall give account."
2. THE PERSONS
   a. The individual aspect
      "every one of us"
   b. The inclusive aspect
      "we must all"
3. THE PURPOSE
   a. The review of our lives
      "give account . . . to God"
   b. The response to our lives
      "that every one may receive the things done in his body"

ILLUSTRATION: Picture two scenes. The first is a law court. A man is on trial for his life. The jury has returned the verdict "Guilty!" and the judge is about to pass the sentence of death. A hush descends as the solemn moment comes. Fear and awe reign in every heart. That's one scene.

Now picture another. It is a flower show and everywhere beautiful plants are on display. The judge arrives. He has a word of praise for almost every exhibit even though just a few are going to win the most coveted prizes. The atmosphere is tinged, perhaps, with some tension, but it is not a matter of life or death, just of reward.

The difference is that in one case a *person* is being judged, in the other case it is *works*.

PAUL'S MISSIONARY VIEWS

ROMANS 15:14-33

He was the greatest missionary of all time. A thorough study of his methods, in the book of Acts for instance, reveals him as a superb missionary statesman and strategist. For one thing he always concentrated on the big cities, planting vigorous churches there and leaving the hinterland for the city church to evangelize. Rome was one city he had not pioneered. Others had that jewel in their crown. Writing to Rome, however, he did not hesitate to spell out his views on mission work, and great views they were!

1. HIS PARISH (15:14-18)
   a. His generous assessment of the Roman Christians (15:14)
   b. His general assumption about the Roman Christians (15:15-18)
      (1) A word of explanation (15:15-16)
          (He claimed Rome as part of his parish.)
      (2) A word of exultation (15:17-18)

2. HIS POWER (15:19)

3. HIS POLICY (15:20-21)
   He had a strategic concept of—
   a. The foe (15:20*a*)
      ("I strived." It is a battle.)
   b. The field (15:20*b*)
   c. The faith (15:21)
      (He based all on Scripture.)

4. HIS PLANS (15:22-29)
   a. Corinth (15:22-23)
   b. Rome (15:24)
   c. Jerusalem (15:25-28)
   d. Spain (15:29)

MARKS OF SPIRITUAL BABYHOOD

1 CORINTHIANS 3:1

"Babes!" There is a note of holy scorn in Paul's use of the word on this occasion. Babies are beautiful and charming in their place. But babes when they should be adults? What a heartache that must be. The Christian life demands constant growth towards maturity. Here are some of the basic characteristics of a babe. None of them is attractive when considered as being a mark of believers who should have grown up long since.

A baby—

1. ALWAYS WANTS ITS OWN WAY
2. CANNOT LEARN DIFFICULT LESSONS
3. IS APT TO QUARREL
4. IS TAKEN UP WITH PERSONALITIES
5. IS POSSESSIVE
6. ALWAYS NEEDS TO BE TAUGHT
7. PLAYS WHILE BIG THINGS ARE HAPPENING
8. HAS NO PROPER SENSE OF VALUES
9. FREQUENTLY SAYS THE WRONG THINGS
10. IS EASILY UPSET

NOTE: A baby is a delightful thing. But a baby thirty years old is a tragedy. Some years ago I was in a park with a friend. A lady approached pushing a buggy in which was the figure of a four or five year old child. I glanced at the little one as they passed and was horrified to see that it had the face of an old woman. My friend said, "That person in the buggy is twenty-five years old." The child had grown old but had never grown up.

THE BELIEVER'S RESURRECTION

1 CORINTHIANS 15

It is no more remarkable that we should live *again* than that we should live *at all*! We just need to think of the bewildering complexity of the human body and the even more intricate workings of the human personality to see that we are indeed "fearfully and wonderfully made" (Ps. 139:14). The God who could make us once can certainly make us again.

1. OUR RESURRECTION BELIEF
   a. It is a fundamental belief
      Apart from it—
      (1) The Word of God is a falsehood
      (2) The work of Christ is a failure
      (3) The witness of the Spirit is a farce
   b. It is a factual belief
      (1) The proof of it: the resurrection of Christ
      (2) The prospect of it: the rapture of the church
   c. It is a fervent belief
      (1) The song of the living and raptured saint: "O death, where is thy sting?"
      (2) The song of the departed but raptured saint: "O grave, where is thy victory?"

2. OUR RESURRECTION BODIES
   a. They are the same bodies
      (Jesus proved that to Thomas)
   b. They are to be splendid bodies
      (this mortal shall put on immortality)
   c. They are to be spirit bodies
      (like His glorious body)

3. OUR RESURRECTION BLISS
   a. We shall be with our Glorious Lord
   b. We shall be in a glorious land

FOUR LAST THINGS

1 CORINTHIANS 15:8, 26, 45, 52

"Last of all," says Paul, "he was seen of me." "The last enemy," he says, "is death." "The last Adam," says Paul, pointing to Christ. "The last trump," he says, reminding us of Christ's second coming. What a great fourfold theme!

1. THE LAST WITNESS (15:8)
   The triumph of His resurrection

2. THE LAST ENEMY (15:26)
   The triumph of His reign

3. THE LAST ADAM (15:45)
   The triumph of His relationship

4. THE LAST TRUMP (15:52)
   The triumph of His return

NOTE: Spurgeon says, "If death is the last enemy, leave him until last." In 1 Corinthians 3:22 Paul says that death is one of God's gifts to His children. We need not fear death; it has been completely disarmed. During the second World War, I served for some time in a camp for prisoners of war. There were thousands of German prisoners in that camp. We were not afraid of them. They had been defeated and disarmed. It is the same with death. It is actually given to us—an enemy, but powerless to harm. It is made to serve us—to usher us into the presence of our Lord and bring us to our eternal home.

A TRANSFORMED LIFE

2 CORINTHIANS 5:14-21

A new creature! That is what it means to be saved. In nine short steps Paul takes us all the way up the glory road. Nine short steps, but nine giant strides! How Paul must have longed for these dear, carnal, worldly, childish Corinthian converts of his to enter into the fulness of it all! How God must long, even yet, for us to enter into the grandeur of it today.

1. MOTIVATION (5:14a)

2. IDENTIFICATION (5:14b)

3. SUBSTITUTION (5:15a)

4. CONSECRATION (5:15b)

5. COMPREHENSION (5:16)

6. TRANSFORMATION (5:17)

7. RECONCILIATION (5:18-19)

8. EVANGELIZATION (5:20)

9. PERFECTION (5:21)

NOTE: Everything hinges on being "in Christ." It is one of Paul's favorite expressions, one he uses in every epistle, one he uses so often that someone has called it "Paul's magnificent obsession." He uses it, or its equivalents, about 170 times. What does it mean? Well, what it meant for Israel to be in the land is what it means for us to be in Christ. All God's blessings for Israel in the Old Testament were in a place. All His blessings for us are in a person.

A NEW CREATURE

2 CORINTHIANS 5:17

"New lamps for old!" You will remember that that was the cry of the old schemer who wished to get his hands on Aladdin's wonderful lamp. The old Arabian story tells how Aladdin discovered a battered old lamp that, upon being rubbed, produced a geni of great power and of complete subservience to the owner of the lamp. With the geni's aid Aladdin became rich and powerful and married to a beautiful princess. His wife did not know the secret of the lamp, so she willingly exchanged the unsightly thing for the shiny new one the caller offered.

"New lives for old!" Only with God it is not a con game but a thrilling, blessed reality. And with that new life comes not a geni but God's blessed Holy Spirit to make all things possible for us. New lives for old! It is the very essence of the gospel. For God does not patch up old lives; He gives new ones.

1. THE TREMENDOUS CHANGE WROUGHT IN A PERSON BY CHRIST
   a. His new position
      "in Christ"
   b. His new personality
      "a new creature"
   c. His new potential
      "all things . . . new"

2. THE TREMENDOUS CHALLENGE BROUGHT TO A PERSON BY CHRIST
   "If"

HOW POOR PEOPLE GIVE

Paul was very proud of these Macedonian friends of his. It was a vision of a man from Macedonia that had turned his missionary feet towards Europe in the first place. The churches of Macedonia had been founded on his second missionary journey. They were located at Philippi, Berea, and Thessalonica. Persecution had driven him out of each one of them in turn. The believers in these cities were, for the most part, poor, despised, and marked for persecution. Yet what noble aristocrats they were when it came to giving! Paul boasts of them to the wealthy, worldly Corinthians and holds them up to all the ages as the greatest of givers.

1. THEY GAVE MAGNANIMOUSLY (8:2)

2. THEY GAVE MUNIFICENTLY (8:3a)

3. THEY GAVE MAGNIFICENTLY (8:3b-4)

4. THEY GAVE METHODICALLY (8:5)

ILLUSTRATION: During the great financial depression of the 1930s a certain wealthy man lost all he had. He had been known as a man who had given royally to the Lord's work in the days of his affluence. Someone asked him, "Don't you wish now you had some of those many thousands you have given away?" "Oh no," he said, "I still have those. In fact that's all I do have now. And I shall have them forever."

61

THOUGH HE WAS RICH

We know He was rich, but we cannot have any idea how rich He really was! The worlds were His, every planet, every star, every galaxy, every speck of cosmic dust. We know He became poor. He was born in a borrowed barn, He needed a borrowed penny, a borrowed boat, a borrowed lunch, a borrowed upper room, a borrowed tomb. He left behind Him just the clothes He wore the day they slew Him. That gives us some measure of how poor He became. We know we shall be rich, indeed, are already rich. But we shall have to wait until we get to heaven to appreciate fully how rich we are.

1. HIS GRACIOUS PERSONALITY
   "Ye know the grace"

2. HIS GREAT PROSPERITY

3. HIS GRINDING POVERTY

4. HIS GLORIOUS PURPOSE
   "That ye . . . might be rich"

NOTE: Ten thousand talents! That was the amount of the debt. The servant in the Lord's parable was appalled at the sum total of his debt. Measured by any standard it was an impossible debt. And it was forgiven him (Matt. 18:23-35). Such is the debt Christ assumed at Calvary—not just for a single individual but for every human being ever to be born on the planet earth.

PAUL IN PRISON

PHILIPPIANS 1:1—2:4

What an irrepressible fellow Paul was! What a constant head-
ache to the devil! Lock him up in prison and he converts his
jailors and takes Caesar's palace by storm! Kill him and you
"promote him to glory," as the Salvationists say. Turn him
loose and he turns the world upside down. But of all the mistakes the devil made in dealing with the church in the first
century, the greatest, surely, was in imprisoning Paul. Out of
that prison of his came Ephesians, Philippians, Colossians and
Philemon, weighty epistles that have been plaguing Satan ever
since.

Prison could not keep Paul from—

1. HIS PEN (1:1-8)

2. HIS PRAYERS (1:9-11)

3. HIS PURPOSE (1:12-18)

4. HIS PROSPECTS (1:19-26)

5. HIS PULPIT (1:27—2:4)

NOTE: The devil does not seem to learn much by his mistakes.
What a mistake he made, for instance, when he shut up John
Bunyan the tinker in that Bedford jail! Out of that jail flowed
a constant stream of writings culminating in *Pilgrim's Prog-
ress,* a book that in its day and for many long years afterwards
was second only to the Bible in sales and influence. Trace out
how many a warrior has sharpened his pencil in prison and
set the world aflame with his words.

THE POWER OF POSITIVE THINKING

PHILIPPIANS 4:1-8

It is an interesting and important fact that we can only think of one thing at a time. Try it and see! Try adding up a long column of figures while, at the same time, paying close attention to something on the radio or T.V. Your mind will simply hop back and forth from one thing to the other with poor results for both. Paul capitalizes on this peculiarity of our minds. He tells us we should fix our thoughts resolutely on certain great positives in order to live a holy life.

The effect of concentration on—

1. THE BELIEVER'S SOCIAL LIFE (4:1-2)

2. THE BELIEVER'S SPIRITUAL LIFE (4:3-5)
   a. It makes him helpful (4:3)
   b. It makes him happy (4:4)
   c. It makes him holy (4:5)

3. THE BELIEVER'S SECULAR LIFE (4:6)

4. THE BELIEVER'S SECRET LIFE (4:7-8)

NOTE: Someone has said "Sow a thought and reap an action, sow an action and reap a habit, sow a habit and reap a character, sow a character and reap an eternal destiny." It is the same principle as that embodied in the old proverb: "For want of a nail a shoe was lost, for want of a shoe a horse was lost, for want of a horse a man was lost, for want of a man a company was lost, for want of a company a battle was lost, for want of a battle a kingdom was lost." It is no wonder that Paul brings us back to basics and says: "Take heed to your thoughts."

THE POWER OF PERPETUAL THANKSGIVING

PHILIPPIANS 4:10-19

Praise is the keynote of Philippians. *Joy* and *rejoicing* are its characteristic words. There was one man in the Philippian assembly who would be rubbing his hands with delighted appreciation as the epistle was being read for the first time. "That's right!" he would exclaim. "Amen! Hallelujah!" And who was he, this brother who was so thrilled over Paul's insistence on joy? Why the Philippian jailor, of course! He and his family had been won to Christ because Paul and Silas, after a thorough beating, had sung hymns of praise until the very earth shook with the sound (Acts 16).

1. THE EXPERIENCES CONNECTED WITH IT (4:10-13)
   The experience of being—
   a. Made to wait (4:10)
   b. Made to want (4:11-12)
   c. Made to win (4:13)

2. THE EXERCISES CONNECTED WITH IT (4:14-19)
   a. On Paul's part (4:14-17)
      (1) His happy memories (4:14-16)
      (2) His honest motives (4:17)
   b. On their part (4:18)
   c. On God's part (4:19)

NOTE: David learned the power of praise. "I will bless the LORD at all times," he said; "his praise shall continually be in my mouth" (Psalm 34:1). Those words were written just after his disastrous flight to Gath, where he had been recognized as the giant-killer and put in fear for his life. He had escaped by pretending to be mad. Yet out of it all he could think of a whole host of things for which to praise the Lord. He resolved that henceforth he would praise God in all circumstances and not allow circumstances to pressure him.

PRAYING FOR OTHER CHRISTIANS

Colossians 1:9-14

What kinds of things should we ask for when we intercede on behalf of other believers? For their success in business? That they might be healed from sickness? That Willie might pass his exams? That it might be a sunny day for Bessie's wedding next week? Maybe! But it would be hard to substantiate many of our prayer requests from Scripture. Paul's prison prayers are most instructive. Here is one of them. Mark well the kinds of things for which he prays on behalf of his Colossian friends.

1. For Spiritual Vision (1:9)
   That they might—
   a. Receive the truth
   b. Realize the truth
   c. Relate the truth

2. For Spiritual Vitality (1:10)
   a. The walk of the Christian life
   b. The works of the Christian life
   c. The wonder of the Christian life

3. For Spiritual Victory (1:11)
   a. Its secret
   b. Its scope

Note: So much of our praying is taken up with the material. Paul lifts prayer to a spiritual dimension. The same is true, of course, with the Lord's prayer. Only one clause ("Give us this day our daily bread") is concerned with the material. When we reach up to God for material things we are invoking his *mercies*; when we pray for spiritual things we are asking for his *blessings*.

66

THE DEITY OF CHRIST

COLOSSIANS 1:15-19

As J. B. Phillips has so expressively phrased it (in the title of his challenging little book) our God is too small. He is not really too small, of course. It is just that our concept of Him is too small. We need to think great thoughts of God. The same is true of the Lord Jesus. He is not merely an outstanding Galilean peasant who happened to have royal blood in His veins and who made a mark on history. He is not merely a man in homespun garb peering at us from the pages of the past. He is the dynamic, omniscient, omnipotent, Creator of the universe. That's who Jesus is.

1. ALL GOD'S PERSONALITY IS CENTERED IN HIM (1:15)
   a. The image of the invisible God
   b. The implication of the incarnate God

2. ALL GOD'S POWER IS CENTERED IN HIM (1:16-17)
   a. He created the universe (1:16a)
   b. He claims the universe (1:16b)
   c. He controls the universe (1:17)

3. ALL GOD'S PURPOSES ARE CENTERED IN HIM (1:18-19)
   a. His absolute sovereignty (1:18a)
   b. His absolute superiority (1:18b)
      (1) He originated life
      (2) He overcame death
   c. His absolute sufficiency (1:19)

THE GOSPEL AND THE CULT

Colossians 2:8-23

Paul had never been to Colosse. The church there had been founded by mission work reaching out from Ephesus or, perhaps, by the labors of one of Paul's friends, possibly his convert Philemon. Two years after this little letter was written the city of Colosse was destroyed by an earthquake. But the letter was not written just for Colosse. It was written for the church of all time. Subtle and dangerous heresies had surfaced at Colosse. A monster with five heads had attacked the church. Paul smote down those heads with the Spirit's mighty sword and, in so doing, has shown us how to deal with similar cultist errors to this very day.

The answer to—

1. Intellectualism (2:8-10

2. Ritualism (2:11-13)

3. Legalism (2:14-17)

4. Mysticism (2:18-19)

5. Asceticism (2:20-23)

Note: The phrase "philosophy and vain deceit" (2:8) is rendered "intellectualism or high-sounding nonsense" by J. B. Phillips in his paraphrase of the New Testament. The best man can say is "I think!" The believer can come back with all the authority of the inspired, infallible, inerrant Word of God and say, "I know!"

FALSE TEACHING EXPOSED

Colossians 2:8-22

Present-day cults have their philosophical roots in ancient
heresies. God saw to it that Satan hurled all he had at the
infant church during the lifetime of the apostles. Thus every
form of lie and falsehood and deviation from the truth of
Christianity could be apostolically answered and refuted in
the New Testament. As a result, Satan has nothing new to
throw at the church. Such books as Galatians, Colossians,
2 Timothy, Hebrews, 2 Peter, and Jude are examples of ancient errors eternally exposed. A good grasp of such books as
these is our best defence against error.

The lie that—

1. Secular Reasoning Can Add to the Gospel (2:8-10)
   a. The meaning of Christ's birth (2:8-9)
   b. The mystery of Christ's body (2:10a)
   c. The majesty of Christ's being (2:10b)

2. Sundry Rituals Can Add to the Gospel (2:11-17)
   a. They cannot sanctify the saint (2:11-13)
   b. They cannot save the sinner (2:14-15)
   c. They cannot satisfy the seeker (2:16-17)

3. Special Revelations Can Add to the Gospel (2:18-19)
   a. The type of modesty they promote (2:18a)
   b. The type of mediator they proclaim (2:18b)
   c. The type of mentality they produce (2:18c-19)

4. Stricter Regulations Can Add to the Gospel (2:20-23)
   a. The falseness of legalism and asceticism (2:20)
   b. The fetters of legalism and asceticism (2:21)
   c. The folly of legalism and asceticism (2:22)

A THREEFOLD CORD

Identification with Christ is an important New Testament concept. When Christ died, I died; when He was buried, I was buried; when He arose, I arose. I was once "dead in sin," but now, because of my identification with Christ, I am "dead to sin." The truth of identification is found in shadow and type in the Old Testament and in explicit statement in the New. It is Paul's major thesis in Romans 6 and it is his continuing theme here. It is what theologians call "positional truth," for it deals with the position we have in Christ. It is translated into practical truth as we grasp its significance and act upon it.

1. OUR SHARE IN CHRIST'S RESURRECTION (3:1a)
   The resurrection of Christ is—
   a. A fact of sacred history
   b. A fact of sound theology
   c. A fact of spiritual experience

2. OUR SHARE IN CHRIST'S RAPTURE (3:1b-3)
   From where He now is He ministers to our need.
   a. His position of strength (3:1b)
      ("where Christ sitteth")
   b. His position of satisfaction (3:2)
      ("set your affection")
   c. His position of security (3:3)
      ("hid with Christ in God")

3. OUR SHARE IN CHRIST'S RETURN (3:4)
   We are to share in—
   a. The life of Christ now
      (He "is our life")
   b. The lordship of Christ then
      ("appear with him")

THE OLD MAN AND THE NEW

COLOSSIANS 3:5-14

Mark Twain introduces us to Huckleberry Finn. After his adoption by the widow Douglas, poor Huckleberry had great difficulty in adjusting to his new life. The problem, of course, was in the matter of his clothes. The poor boy was far too attached to that picturesque ruin of rags that had made him such a colorful figure in the community before he struck it rich. He had great difficulty both in donning and in wearing his new clothes. In the Bible, of course, clothes symbolize habits. "Off with the old," says God, "on with the new! Off with the old, at once and once for all."

1. THE OLD MAN (3:5-9)
    a. The old man's ruin (3:5-7)
        (1) Its reality (3:5a)
        (2) Its roots (3:5b)
        (3) Its remedy (3:6-7)
    b. The old man's rags (3:8-9)
        (1) His evil whims (3:8a)
        (2) His evil words (3:8b-9a)
        (3) His evil ways (3:9b)

2. THE NEW MAN (3:10-14)
    a. The new man's righteousness (3:10-11)
    b. The new man's robes (3:12-14)
        We are to put on—
        (1) Goodness (3:12)
        (2) Graciousness (3:13)
        (3) Godliness (3:14)

THE CHRISTIAN HOME

A manufacturer of a product ought to know best how to make his product perform. If the instructions say: "Press button 'A' before pressing button 'B,' " there has to be a reason for the procedure. The order is bound to be important. We can have little cause for complaint if we ignore his instructions and do as we please. If his product refuses to function aright we can blame only ourselves so long as we are ignoring its maker's instructions. Now marriage was God's invention. His instructions for its proper performance are found in His Word. We had best heed them if marriage is to work smoothly and well.

1. WIVES: BE RESPECTFUL (3:18)
    "Submit," if you want—
    a. A healthy marriage
    b. A happy marriage
    c. A holy marriage

2. HUSBANDS: BE REGARDFUL (3:19)
    "Love," if you want God's best.
    a. Be the sovereign in your home
    b. Be the sweetheart in your home

3. CHILDREN: BE RELIABLE (3:20)
    "Obey."
    a. The extent of this obedience
    b. The example of this obedience
    c. The excellence of this obedience

4. FATHERS: BE REASONABLE (3:21)
    "Provoke not." Pay attention to—
    a. The way you demand obedience
    b. Why you demand obedience
    c. When you demand obedience

THE CHRISTIAN BUSINESSMAN

Colossians 3:22—4:1

Unions would never have been dreamed of had employees and employers heeded God's laws for management and employment. The Christian employer should be the most generous, considerate, desirable employer in the community. The Christian employee should be the most conscientious, hardworking, dependable man on the payroll. Unfortunately it does not always happen like that, but that's the way it would be if the Golden Rule of Scripture were applied to business relations.

1. How an Employee Must Behave (3:22-25)
   a. The measure of his service (3:22a)
   b. The manner of his service (3:22b-23)
      Supervisors should be able to
      (1) Load him to capacity (3:22b)
      (2) Leave him with confidence (3:23)
   c. The motive of his service (3:24-25)
      Paul lifts secular employment to—
      (1) The eternal plane (3:24a)
      (2) The evangelical plane (3:24b)
      (3) The ethical plane (3:25)

2. How an Employer Must Behave (4:1)
   a. He is a man in authority
   b. He is a man under authority

Note: "Ye serve the Lord Christ!" The word was addressed to *slaves*. It lifted all servitude, all bondage, all employment to a higher plane. "Your actual employer is Christ" is the way one translater paraphrases it.

THE CHRISTIAN NEIGHBOR

Colossians 4:2-6

Are you nice to know? All too often the Christian has a problem of relating to his neighbors. He may be afraid, perhaps, of getting involved in something worldly. Perhaps he has distorted ideas of what is meant by "separation" for the Christian. In the Bible separation is never isolation; it is insulation. The Christian should be like a live wire, well insulated by his position "in Christ," in touch with the power at one end and in touch with the need at the other. Here's how it works.

1. Be Prayerful in Character (4:2-4)
   Prayer is to be—
   a. The great habit of life
      "Continue"
   b. The guarded habit of life
      "Watch"
   c. The grateful habit of life
      "Thanksgiving"
   d. The grandest habit of life
      "For us" (a share in Paul's ministry)

2. Be Prudent in Conduct (4:5)
   a. Guard your testimony (4:5a)
   b. Guard your time (4:5b)

3. Be Pungent in Conversation (4:6)
   Put some—
   a. Pleasantness into your conversation
      "With grace"
   b. Punch into your conversation
      "Seasoned with salt"
   c. Point into your conversation
      "Know how ye ought to answer"

THE COMING GREAT APOSTASY

2 Thessalonians 2:3-12

Paul's second letter to the Thessalonians was occasioned by error. False teachings about the second coming of Christ were circulating. A forged letter bearing Paul's name was giving added weight to the teachings. The believers were being further deceived by "prophetic" pronouncements and by "spirit" utterances. It was a threefold cord of deception. Paul used the occasion of this local deception at Thessalonica as a springboard to launch into an exposure of Satan's deepest plans for the end-time deception of most of mankind.

1. How the Man of Sin Is Revealed (2:3-4)
    a. The unveiling of Satan's man (2:3)
    b. The unmasking of Satan's plan (2:4)

2. How the Mystery of Iniquity Is Restrained (2:5-7)

3. How the Might of Satan Is Released (2:8-12)
    a. By divine permission (2:8-10)
    b. For eternal perdition (2:11-12)

Note: The passage has to do with the coming "day of the Lord." In 2 Thessalonians 2:2 reference is made to "the day of Christ." It is generally agreed that the phrase should be translated "the day of the Lord." The day of Christ is referred to in verse 1 and has to do with the coming of the Lord for His church. The day of the Lord was the subject of extensive Old Testament revelation and embraces the great period that stretches from the rapture down through the Kingdom age.

A FAITHFUL SAYING

1 Timothy 1:15

Paul was an intellectual, probably the greatest of them all. He had not always believed the gospel of Christ. At one time he had been a radical unbeliever. But Paul had become so convinced of the truth of the gospel that he had launched his whole life on a vast crusade to convince others. Basically, of course, the gospel appeal is to the heart. At the same time it is thoroughly sane and logical. Nobody has to commit intellectual suicide in order to become a Christian.

1. The Credibility of the Gospel
   "This is a faithful saying" ("This statement is completely reliable"—J. B. Phillips)

2. The Content of the Gospel
   a. The record of Christ's coming
      "Christ Jesus came"
   b. The reason for Christ's coming
      "to save sinners"

3. The Claims of the Gospel
   "Worthy of all acceptation" ("should be universally accepted"—J. B. Phillips)

Note: This is the first of five "faithful sayings" in the pastoral epistles. Compare 1 Timothy 3:1; 4:9; 2 Timothy 2:11; and Titus 3:8. The word for "saying" is *logos*, the Word. In the last analysis God brings man back to the point of original departure. The race departed from God by refusing to put full credence in His word, trusting instead the lies of the serpent. Salvation and damnation hinge on one's attitude to God's faithful sayings, true words.

PAUL'S CHURCH LETTERS

2 TIMOTHY 3:16-17

Paul wrote to seven churches, as did John. The order in which Paul's church letters appear in the New Testament is full of instruction. They group themselves around the great theme of 2 Timothy 3:16-17. They have to do with doctrine, reproof, and correction. A survey of the letters to these seven churches in the order in which they are arranged in the New Testament is most instructive. The theme begins with the gospel (Romans) and ends with the glory (Thessalonians). No reproof and no correction follow Thessalonians, for after Christ's coming there will be no more need for either.

1. THE MYSTERY OF CHRIST'S CROSS
   a. Romans:
      the doctrine of the cross
   b. Corinthians:
      reproof for moral departure from the truth of Romans
   c. Galatians:
      correction for doctrinal departure from the truth of Romans

2. THE MYSTERY OF CHRIST'S CHURCH
   a. Ephesians:
      the doctrine of the church
   b. Philippians:
      reproof for moral departure from the truth of Ephesians
   c. Colossians:
      correction for doctrinal departure from the truth of Ephesians

3. THE MYSTERY OF CHRIST'S COMING
   Thessalonians:
   The doctrine of the coming

A NOTE ABOUT SLAVERY

PHILEMON

The great social problem of Paul's day was slavery. There were more slaves than there were citizens and freed men in the vast empire of Rome, many more. Slaves had no rights. An irate master could flog or torture, maim or kill a slave with complete impunity. Runaway slaves were scourged and crucified if caught. Other slaveowners took it for granted that a master would treat an escaped slave in this way. Philemon was a slaveowner; he was also a Christian. Onesimus was a runaway slave of his, led to Christ in far-off Rome. How Paul dealt with this horrendous social problem is of great interest. It forms the theme of this little memo to Philemon, carried to him by the returning Onesimus. The epistle exemplifies the way for treating all social problems—in spiritual terms.

1. AN INJURY
   Onesimus had robbed his master.

2. AN INTERCESSOR
   Paul comes between the sinner and his wronged lord.

3. AN INJUNCTION
   Onesimus must return to his wronged master.

4. AN INFLUENCE
   He is to return in Paul's name and for Christ's sake.

5. AN INDEBTEDNESS
   Paul says: "I will repay."

6. AN INSURANCE
   Onesimus returned a changed man.

7. AN INTENTION
   He is now "a brother beloved."

NOTE: It is not hard to see a gospel application in this whole story.

THY THRONE, O GOD

HEBREWS 1:8-9

Jesus is God in the absolute sense of the word. He claimed to be God. The New Testament says He is God. The Old Testament heralded Him as God. Any denial or dilution of His deity is heresy. The deity of Christ is a stumbling block to the Jews as it is to Jehovah's Witnesses and all other cults. Face all who deny His deity with Hebrews 1:8-9. Trumpet loud this truth. Jesus is not a son of God in the sense that all men are sons of God (as some falsely claim). He is God, over all, blessed for evermore. He is God the Son, second person of the Godhead, uncreated and self-existing.

1. THE SOVEREIGNTY OF CHRIST
   "thy throne"

2. THE DEITY OF CHRIST
   "O God"

3. THE DYNASTY OF CHRIST
   "for ever and ever"

4. THE AUTHORITY OF CHRIST
   "the sceptre"

5. THE INTEGRITY OF CHRIST
   "righteousness"

6. THE SPIRITUALITY OF CHRIST
   "God . . . hath anointed"

7. THE VIVACITY OF CHRIST
   "the oil of gladness"

CHRIST'S GREAT OFFERING

HEBREWS 10:10, 19

The body of Jesus! The blood of Jesus! Every time we spread the table and set out the emblems we focus our attention on both. Who can measure the value of the body and the blood? God prized that body. He refused to allow corruption to touch it in the tomb. After Christ's death none but loving hands were allowed to touch it. God prized the blood. He calls it "the precious blood of Christ" (1 Pet. 1:19).

1. THE BODY OF JESUS (10:10)

   Christ has—

   a. A mystical body: the church
   b. A memorial body: the loaf on the table
   c. A material body: His physical body in which He suffered and in which He is now enthroned on high.

2. THE BLOOD OF JESUS (10:19)
   a. Its Value: sin is shown in Scripture to be—
      (1) A disease that only blood can cure
      (2) A debt that only blood can cancel
      (3) A defilement that only blood can cleanse
   b. Its Virtue: it brings us nigh to God

CHRIST OUR PRIEST

HEBREWS 10:11-12

The priest has always wielded enormous power amongst men.
God, in His wisdom, separated "church and state" in Israel by
limiting the priesthood to the family of Aaron and true sovereignty to the family of David. Hebrews speaks much of the
priesthood of the Lord Jesus. He is the only royal priest Israel
will ever have. Today He is our great High Priest, and what
a wonderful, capable priest He is! All religious systems in
Christendom today which ordain priests patently ignore the
teaching of Hebrews.

1. HIS PERSON (10:12a)

2. HIS PASSION (10:11-12b)

3. HIS POSITION (10:12c)

NOTE: "Every priest standeth . . ., but this man . . . sat down."
In the holy place of the tabernacle there was a table, but no
chairs. The Old Testament priests had an unfinished work.
From generation to generation it went on. The only priest in
the Old Testament we see sitting down was old Eli—and what
a wretched failure he was. The first time you see him he's
sitting by a post of the tabernacle. The next time he's in bed
and a little boy has to awaken him. The last time he's by the
wayside, sitting on a seat from which he falls and breaks his
neck. But the Lord Jesus, our great High Priest, sits down.
He sits in the conscious knowledge that redemption's work is
done.

81

MARKS OF THE NEW BIRTH

1 JOHN

It is a dictum with some people that in order to be sure we have been born again we should be able to state the place where, the time when, and the manner how it happened. Not all of us, though, can be that precise. Nor is it necessary. How does a person know he was born? Nobody can recall the details of his natural birth. But any person knows he was born by the simple and evident fact that he is alive! Just so with the new birth. It is not knowing how, when, or where that matters. It is being spiritually alive. John deals with this and gives us half a dozen tests.

1. THE MARK OF SPIRITUAL DEPORTMENT (2:29)

2. THE MARK OF SPIRITUAL DESIRE (3:9)

3. THE MARK OF SPIRITUAL DISPOSITION (4:7)

4. THE MARK OF SPIRITUAL DISCERNMENT (5:1)

5. THE MARK OF SPIRITUAL DELIVERANCE (5:4)

6. THE MARK OF SPIRITUAL DOMINION (5:18)

NOTE: The phrase "born again" has suddenly passed into the vernacular. The testimonies of men like Charles Colson and the enormous popularity of his autobiography have popularized the phrase. This makes it all the more imperative that we teach what the Bible teaches about the new birth. No empty profession of faith will do, no counterfeit pseudo-spiritual experience. If one's experience of being born again does not produce the kind of life John describes, it is suspect.

AS HE IS, SO ARE WE IN THIS WORLD

1 JOHN 4:17

Nine monosyllables! Just nine little words in the simplest possible form of speech. It is part of the genius of the Bible that the profoundest concepts are often conveyed in the simplest of ways. Pick them up, these translucent pearls of wisdom all strung out in a row, turn them this way and that, examine them, prize them, wear them. Let them adorn with their beauty the robe of righteousness Christ gives.

1. THE PLAN: AS HE IS!
   a. A transformed life
      (Christ's incarnation changed the mode of His life. He is now, forever, the *man* Christ Jesus.)
   b. A triumphant life
      (Trace the Lord's constant victories.)

2. THE PLEDGE: SO ARE WE!
   a. A transformed life
      (As Christ took our kind of life, so we take His.)
   b. A triumphant life
      (We can be victorious too.)

3. THE PLACE: IN THIS WORLD!
   (God wants us to live the Christ-life here and now.)

ILLUSTRATION: Read the story of Elijah and Elisha in 2 Kings 2. Elisha wanted a double portion of Elijah's spirit. He fulfilled the conditions and obtained what he desired. Then we have a man in the glory and a man on earth. The man on earth is living the life of the man in the glory, and as a result he does even greater works than the man now in the glory had done when he had been on earth.

CHRISTIAN LIVING

1 PETER

Peter, James, and John all seem to have the same picturesque style of presenting truth which so marked the Master. Peter's first epistle, for instance, abounds with word pictures and allusions to his own experiences as a disciple of the Lord. It abounds with similies. Here is a round half dozen of them, each of which is fascinating.

1. AS SHEEP GOING ASTRAY (2:25)

2. AS NEWBORN BABES (2:2)

3. AS OBEDIENT CHILDREN (1:14)

4. AS STRANGERS AND PILGRIMS (2:11)

5. AS LIVING STONES (2:5)

6. AS GOOD STEWARDS (3:10)

ILLUSTRATION: A sheep is neither swift nor strong nor smart. Its chief characteristic is that it is stupid. If there is a hole in the hedge and one sheep goes through, the whole flock will follow. And once away from the fold a sheep is at the mercy of its foes. It is not like a dog, which can find its own way back. A sheep simply does not have the capacity to find its own way home. When Peter says "Ye . . . are now returned unto the Shepherd," he means that the Shepherd had sought and found the lost sheep and brought it back Himself. There is a great difference here between the Old and New Testaments. In the Old Testament the sheep was slain for the shepherd—witness the blood-red altars of Israel. But in the New Testament, the Shepherd was slain for the sheep—the great message of Calvary.

THE GREAT BENEDICTION

Revelation 1:5-6

The book of Revelation begins more like a Pauline epistle than a great apocalypse of judgment. It begins with a blessing and with a benediction. The word *apocalypse,* so often applied to the Revelation, means "unveiling." It is an apt descriptive word, for above all else this book unveils the glories of the Lord Jesus Christ. Again and again, in this opening chapter for instance, our attention is drawn back to Him. Like John, we should never get tired of gazing on the Lord in His glory.

1. The Grace That Accrues to Us
   a. The Father's compassionate work
      "Unto him that loved us"
   b. The Son's cleansing work
      "Washed us from our sins"
   c. The Spirit's converting work
      "Made us kings and priests"

2. The Glory That Accrues to Him
   a. Personal glory
      "Unto him"
   b. Positional glory
      "Glory and dominion"
   c. Perpetual glory
      "For ever and ever"

Note: That phrase "for ever and ever" runs like a refrain from beginning to end of the Apocalypse. Trace it out—1:6; 4:9, 10; 5:13, 14; 7:12; 10:6; 11:15; 14:11; 15:17; 20:10; 22:5. The phrase literally means "to the ages of the ages."

THE UNVEILED CHRIST

REVELATION 1:13-18

John once pillowed his head on Jesus' breast. But not now!
"I . . . heard," he says, "I turned," "I saw," "I fell at his feet
as dead." He saw the Christ in all His awesome power emerg-
ing for judgment. Yet it was "this same Jesus," the beloved
Saviour he had known long since. "Fear not!" He said. And
all John's fears melted like snow before a summer's sun.
Thereafter, through all the length of the book, amidst scenes
that might well awe the stoutest heart, John moves unafraid.
The throne, the cherubim, the elders, the crash of empire, the
thunders of God's wrath—none of these can stir again the
slightest tremor in his soul.

1. How Glorious He Is (1:13-16)
    a. Unknowable (1:13a)
       "Clothed . . . down to the foot" (completely concealed)
    b. Unemotional (1:13b)
       "Girt about the paps"
    c. Unimpeachable (1:14a)
       "His head and his hairs . . . like . . . snow"
    d. Undeterrable (1:15a)
       "His feet like unto fine brass"
    e. Unanswerable (1:15b)
       "His voice as the sound of many waters"
    f. Unparalleled (1:16a)
       "In his right hand seven stars"
    g. Unconquerable (1:16b)
       "Out of his mouth . . . a . . . sword"
    h. Undeceivable (1:14b)
       "His eyes were as a flame of fire"
    i. Unapproachable (1:16c)
       "His countenance . . . as the sun"

2. How Gracious He Is (1:17)

3. How Great He Is (1:18)

THE SEVEN CHURCHES

REVELATION 2-3

There were more than seven churches in the Roman province of Asia Minor. There were Colosse and Hierapolis, for instance, not mentioned at all by John. The seven churches addressed were doubtless selected by the risen Lord because of the conditions they embodied. The letters contain *practical* instruction. That is, they were addressed to seven churches then in existence to remedy conditions that then prevailed. The letters contain *perennial* instruction, for the conditions that existed in these seven churches have existed in churches from that day to this. The letters contain *prophetic* instruction, for, as many have pointed out, taken in the order in which they are addressed, the seven churches give us seven cameos of the entire church age.

1. THE FORMAL CHURCH
   Ephesus

2. THE FEARFUL CHURCH
   Smyrna

3. THE FALTERING CHURCH
   Pergamos

4. THE FALSE CHURCH
   Thyatira

5. THE FAMOUS CHURCH
   Sardis

6. THE FAITHFUL CHURCH
   Philadelphia

7. THE FASHIONABLE CHURCH
   Laodicea

BEHOLD, I STAND AT THE DOOR, AND KNOCK

REVELATION 3:20

Theologians are quick to point out that this text belongs with its context. Thus placed it evidently shows us a church so far from what God ever planned for His church that Christ is actually outside the whole thing—shut out and seeking entrance. Granted! But it is with true spiritual insight that preachers have seized on this text and used it, purely and simply, as a gospel text. Christ is seen shut out of a human life, knocking, calling, promising.

1. CHRIST'S SOBERING POSITION:
   Outside. "Behold, I stand . . . and knock"

2. CHRIST'S SIMPLE PLEA:
   "If any man hear my voice"

3: CHRIST'S SOLEMN PROMISE:
   a. He promises to save
      "I will come in to him"
   b. He promises to sanctify
      "I . . . will sup with him"
   c. He promises to secure
      "And he with me"

ILLUSTRATION: In St. Paul's Cathedral, London, there hangs a famous painting entitled *The Light of the World*. It depicts Christ standing outside a fast-closed door—a door all overgrown with weeds—and patiently seeking admission. When that painting was first hung the critics came to review it. One of them said to the artist, Holman Hunt, "Mr. Hunt you have painted a magnificent picture. But you have made a terrible mistake. You have painted *no handle* on that door." The artist replied, "That is no mistake my friend, the handle is on the *inside.*"

THE HEAVENLY COURT

These two chapters focus on the throne of God. They give us one of the great glimpses we have of heaven in the Bible. They show us something of those "wheels within wheels" that revolve in the unseen world and effect the destinies of men. Before any of the devastating judgments take place in the Apocalypse, the wheels begin to turn in heaven. In this portion we see something of the majestic calm of heaven's court as proceedings are begun to deal with the rebel planet earth. As Daniel taught Nebuchadnezzar, "The heavens do rule" (Dan. 4:26).

1. THE COURT (Rev. 4:1-2)

2. THE CREATOR (4:3)

3. THE COUNCIL (4:4-5)

4. THE CHERUBIM (4:6-11)

5. THE CHARTER (5:1)

6. THE CHALLENGE (5:2-4)

7. THE CHAMPION (5:5-7)

8. THE CHORUS (5:8-14)

NOTE: The scroll was the title deed of earth. The only person ever born on this planet and fit to take that scroll is the Lord Jesus. The events that follow in the Apocalypse all stem from the transfer of that scroll into the Lord's hand. As He breaks the seals, the subsequent judgments sweep the globe. The world is His—His by right of creation, His by right of Calvary, and as this vision shows, His by right of conquest. Not for one moment has He surrendered the planet to His foes.

THE FIRST BEAST

REVELATION 13:1-10

There are two beasts, one is political, the other religious; one arises out of the sea (the nations), the other out of the earth (Israel); one is a Gentile, the other a Jew. They stand shoulder to shoulder to usher in Satan's empire on earth and to bring that age-old "mystery of iniquity" (2 Thess. 2:7) to its final head. The first beast of Revelation 13 appears to be identical with the man of sin of 2 Thessalonians 2.

1. HE DEFIES THE LORD (13:5-6)

2. HE DESTROYS THE SAINTS (13:7)

3. HE DECEIVES THE WORLD (13:8-9)

4. HE DOOMS THE EMPIRE (13:10)

NOTE: The beast has two comings. His first coming is from the sea, the second is from the abyss. When he first comes he will be an ordinary human being—a dazzling genius, demon possessed, no doubt, but a real human being. But he is killed, as Revelation 17 shows, and he has a second coming. This time he is the beast out of the abyss—no longer quite human but a supernatural being determined to force the world to worship both him and his mentor, Satan. His savage policies eventually cause the eastern segment of his empire to break away and precipitate the events that culminate in Armageddon. The world today is awaiting the coming of such a seeming saviour, one who will start out by solving its problems and bringing in prosperity and peace.

THE GREAT WHITE THRONE

REVELATION 20:11-15

There are a number of judgments described in Scripture. There is the judgment of sin at the cross, the judgment of the believer in this life and again at the judgment seat of Christ, the judgment of the living nations, and this judgment—the judgment of the wicked dead at the great white throne.

1. THE FEARFUL SIGHT
   a. The seat of all power:
      the throne
   b. The source of all power:
      He "that sat on it"
   c. The sign of all power:
      a banished universe

2. THE FINAL SUMMONS
   a. The presence of the wicked dead is required at this judgment
   b. The past of the wicked dead is reviewed at this judgment
      It is—
      (1) Total judgment
          "small and great"
      (2) Truthful judgment
          "the books were opened"
      (3) Terrible judgment
          "according to their works"

3. THE FATAL SENTENCE
   a. The final prison:
      "death and hell were cast into the lake of fire"
   b. The final punishment:
      "whosoever was not found written"

GOD'S DEALINGS WITH MEN

God has not always dealt with men on the same terms. From time to time He has changed His approach. There are some nine clearly discernible time spans in the Scriptures. During each of these God has dealt with the human race in a different way. Each of the periods ends in judgment and is followed by a new beginning. Occasionally there is a period of overlap from one age to the other, but frequently the break is sudden and sharp.

1. INNOCENCE (Gen. 1:28–3:13)

2. CONSCIENCE (Gen. 3:22–7:23)
Every man did "his own thing." This resulted in conditions that demanded the Flood.

3. HUMAN GOVERNMENT (Gen. 8:20–11:9)

4. PROMISE (Gen. 12:1–Exod. 19:8)

5. LAW (Exod. 19:8–Matt. 27:35)

6. GRACE (Acts 1–Rev. 3)
God's grace has always been extended to men. In this age, however, all is of grace, in contrast with the previous age, when Law and works predominated.

7. JUDGMENT (Rev. 4-19)

8. KINGDOM (Rev. 20:1-3)

9. ETERNITY (Rev. 20-21)

NOTE: Some divide up these periods in a slightly different way. However, a literal, grammatical, cultural approach to Bible interpretation will necessitate the recognition of the fact that there are well-defined periods in God's dealings with men and that God's administration has by no means been the same from one to another of them.

THE WORK OF THE HOLY SPIRIT

Much confusion exists about the person and work of the Holy Spirit because of careless exegesis and flippant use of Bible terms. For instance, the baptism of the Spirit is referred to directly only seven times in the New Testament. The first five references are prophetic (Matt. 3:11; Mark 1:8; Luke 3:16; John 1:26, 33; Acts 1:5) and refer to John's preaching. One is historical (Acts 11:16) and only one is doctrinal (1 Cor. 12:13). It is this last reference that gives us the spiritual significance of the baptism. It has nothing to do with tongues or super-holiness. It has to do with placing people as members into the mystical body of Christ.

1. MYSTICAL
   a. I am now in Christ: the baptism (1 Cor. 12:13)
   b. Christ is now in me:
      (1) The gift (Acts 2:38)
      (2) The indwelling (1 Cor. 3:16; 6:19)

2. MOTIVATIONAL
   a. The present: the seal (Eph. 1:13)
      "You are eternally mine"
   b. The prospect: the earnest (Eph. 1:14)
      "I am eternally yours"

3. MINISTERIAL
   a. To make me spiritual: the filling (Eph. 5:18)
   b. To make me successful: the anointing (1 John 2:20)

THE NAMES AND NATURE OF THE HOLY SPIRIT

God characteristically reveals Himself by His names and titles. Elohim, Adonai, Jehovah (with their compounds) were names by which He revealed Himself to Israel. Think of the matchless names and titles of the Lord Jesus Christ which abound in Scripture! In keeping with this, God tells us much about His Holy Spirit by the names and titles by which He is addressed. Each one reveals another facet of His character and of the ministry He wishes to perfect in our hearts.

1. THE SPIRIT OF TRUTH (John 14:17)
   I should never be *deceived*.

2. THE SPIRIT OF FAITH (2 Cor. 4:13)
   I should never be *discouraged*.

3. THE SPIRIT OF GRACE (Heb. 10:29)
   I should never be *disgruntled*.

4. THE SPIRIT OF HOLINESS (Rom. 1:4)
   I should never be *defiled*.

5. THE SPIRIT OF WISDOM (Eph. 1:17)
   I should never be *daunted*.

6. THE SPIRIT OF POWER (2 Tim. 1:7)
   I should never be *defeated*.

7. THE SPIRIT OF LOVE (2 Tim. 1:7)
   I should never be *discordant*.

8. THE SPIRIT OF A SOUND MIND (2 Tim. 1:7)
   I should never be *disturbed*.

9. THE SPIRIT OF LIFE (Rom. 8:2)
   I should never be *dead*.

10. THE SPIRIT OF GLORY (1 Pet. 4:14)
    I should never be *dull*.

NOTE: Each of these characteristics is a characteristic of the Lord Jesus. This shows that the Spirit's great work is not to draw attention to Himself but to magnify Christ.

THE ANOINTING OF THE SPIRIT

In the Old Testament, prophets, priests, and kings were all anointed with oil for their ministry. Such symbolic anointings were figurative and anticipated the coming of the Lord Jesus, who was to be God's Messiah (Christ, Anointed). In Him the three great offices merged and had their fullest blaze of glory. Ever filled with the Holy Spirit, the Lord Jesus was anointed by the Spirit of God just prior to the commencement of His public ministry. John refers to our "unction," or anointing. The implication to be derived from his use of the terms is that we are anointed by the Spirit so that we can use God's Word with discernment and power.

1. THE OLD TESTAMENT ANOINTING
   a. For certain specific occupations
      (1) The priest: for virtue (Exod. 29:7)
      (2) The prophet: for vision (1 Kings 19:16)
      (3) The prince: for victory (1 Sam. 15:1)
   b. For certain specific occasions
      (1) For strength—Samson (Judg. 14:6, 19)
      (2) For skill—to build the tabernacle (Exod. 35:30-35)

2. THE NEW TESTAMENT ANOINTING
   a. The anointing of the Christ (Luke 4:18)
   b. The anointing of the Christian (1 John 2:20, 27)
      (1) The occupational anointing: to know how, when, and where to open the Scriptures
      (2) The occasional anointing: for specific and exceptional ministry (that of Charles Finney and D. L. Moody, for instance)

THE HOLY SPIRIT AND THE WORLD

Christianity is a supernatural encounter from beginning to end. It is centered in a supernatural person, the Lord Jesus. It begins with a supernatural experience known as the new birth. It is made possible by the supernatural ministries of the Holy Spirit. Its great teachings are contained in a supernatural book, the Bible. The church is a supernatural invasion of time, born in a supernatural event on the day of Pentecost and to be withdrawn by a supernatural event at the rapture. It is the Holy Spirit who dominates this age. He it is who imparts divine life to a dead soul. He it is who holds back the flood tides of human wickedness and who, from time to time, brings in tremendous spiritual revivals. He sustains a three-fold ministry towards the unregenerate world of men.

1. HIS RESTRAINING MINISTRY (2 Thess. 2:7)

2. HIS REPROVING MINISTRY (John 16:8)
   a. Of the nature of sin
   b. Of the need for righteousness
   c. Of the nearness of judgment

3. HIS REGENERATING MINISTRY (John 3:6)

NOTE: In 2 Thessalonians 2:7 the word "letteth" is an old English word better translated "hindereth." It is a word that has drastically changed its meaning since the King James Version was translated. The hinderer of verses 6-7 is clearly the Holy Spirit. The restrainer is referred to in the neuter in verse 6 and in the masculine in verse 7. Only the Spirit of God can be referred to thus.

THREE DIMENSIONS OF PRAYER

Private prayer has its rules. One of them is the rule of secrecy and quiet. Thus it is that the Lord instructs us to seek out our "closet" when we pray. That is, we are to find a place where we can be as free from distraction as possible—not always easy in our crowded, noisy world. Satan has a vested interest in keeping us from praying. That is why we experience such a struggle both in starting and in persevering with the business of prayer. God has made spiritual provision for us in the armor He has provided. When we finally "break through" we reach that place of which the hymn-writer spoke—that "place of quiet rest, near to the heart of God," where true worship and prayer begin.

1. THE HIDDEN PLACES (Matt. 6:6)
   Places of deliberate withdrawal

2. THE HEAVENLY PLACES (Eph. 6:11-18)
   Places of demonic war
   a. The Adversaries (6:12)
   b. The Armor (6:13-17)
   c. The Attitude (6:18)

3. THE HOLY PLACES
   Places of divine worship
   a. The holy place
      In the divine precincts
   b. The holy of holies
      In the divine presence

A CRISIS AGE

ZECHARIAH 4:6; ESTHER 4:14; JOHN 14:3

We are living in a momentous day in this world's history. On every hand the signs of the Lord's imminent return are multiplying. The next event on God's political calendar is the home-call of the church, to be followed by a rush of events each of which will fulfill this or that prophetic utterance. The fact that scores of old prophecies are now awake and clamoring for the fulfillment surely heralds the coming of the end. There are three alternatives ahead.

1. RUIN

   In today's world this possibility is written large on the front page of almost every newspaper and paraded before us daily on our television screens.

2. REVIVAL

   God could send a spiritual awakening that would postpone things for another generation. There seems to be little sign of this. Probably the next great spiritual awakening will be that second Pentecost which will follow the rapture of the church and fulfill all of Joel's predictions.

3. RAPTURE

   So far as the church is concerned, there remains not a single shred of prophecy to be fulfilled before its withdrawal from the scene.

98

THIS MAN

"This man!" How much the Bible so often packs into a phrase. What delightful fields of study are opened up to the searching soul by the pursuit of such a phrase up and down the byways of the Word! Think of what the Bible has to say about "this man!" "Never man spake like this man." "I find no fault in this man." "This man receiveth sinners."

1. His CONVERSATION (John 7:46)

2. His COMPASSION (Luke 15:2)

3. His CONDUCT (Luke 23:41)

4. His CAREER (John 11:47)

5. His COMPREHENSION (John 7:15)

6. His CLAIMS (John 6:52)

7. His CONQUEST (Heb. 10:12)

NOTE: Christianity is Christ! We cannot be too much occupied with Him. It is to be feared that today the great emphasis has moved away from Christ to the Holy Spirit. Yet the Holy Spirit's great work is to exalt the Lord Jesus Christ (see John 16:13-14 and compare v. 15 and also 14:26 and 15:26). Any movement that emphasizes the Holy Spirit out of all proportion and is more occupied with Him than with the Lord Jesus is suspect. The Holy Spirit does have an important role in God's purposes for this age, but He keeps Himself in the background and draws our attention to Christ. Christ-centered preaching is the vital need of the hour.

HOW GOD NAMES HIS PEOPLE

In the New Testament we do not meet Baptists, Congregationalists, Methodists, or Presbyterians. We do not meet Salvationists, Pentecostals, or Plymouth Brethren. Instead we meet believers, brethren, disciples, Christians, saints. The titles by which God calls His people are all universal in scope and definitive in character. They are intended to emphasize a great New Testament truth. All born-again believers belong to the same universal church. It is a truth worth remembering, especially when we find ourselves closing heart, mind, and compassion to others who love the Lord.

1. BELIEVERS (Acts 5:14; 1 Tim. 4:12)
   This describes their *convictions*

2. BRETHREN (Acts 6:3; Rom. 12:1)
   This describes their *company*

3. DISCIPLES (Acts 9:1; 20:7)
   This describes their *commitment*

4. CHRISTIANS (Acts 11:26; 1 Pet. 4:16)
   This describes their *conduct*

5. SAINTS (Acts 9:13; Rom. 1:7)
   This describes their *character*

NOTE: The Roman Catholic idea that only super-holy people, subsequently canonized by the Roman Catholic Church, are saints is plainly unscriptural. The word is used in the New Testament to describe all those who have put their faith and trust in the Lord Jesus.

THE DOCTRINE OF SALVATION

Some years ago a man in a penitentiary studied a Moody correspondence course. He found Christ. In answer to one of the questions which gave him an opportunity to express where he stood in relation to his newfound faith, he wrote down: "I am a new man in an old body." It was a most perceptive remark. For that is what salvation is. But it will go even further than that saved prisoner realized. One day he will be a new man in a new body.

1. REPENTANCE: A CHANGE OF MIND (Matt. 3:8)

2. REGENERATION: A CHANGE OF HEART (John 3:3)

3. CONVERSION: A CHANGE OF LIFE (Matt. 18:3)

4. ADOPTION: A CHANGE OF FAMILY (Rom. 8:14-17)

5. SANCTIFICATION: A CHANGE OF BEHAVIOR (Heb. 10:14-16)

6. JUSTIFICATION: A CHANGE OF STATE (Rom. 5:1)

7. GLORIFICATION: A CHANGE OF PLACE (John 17:24)

ILLUSTRATION: Justified! In popular, everyday language the word can be paraphrased: "just as if I'd never sinned!"

Some years ago a wealthy Englishman bought a Rolls Royce car and took it to France on his vacation. It broke down. At great expense the factory flew out a mechanic and not only repaired the car but entertained the customer in the best available hotel. When he arrived home he expected to receive a large bill but none came. Eventually he wrote, asking for his account to be rendered. He received this reply: "Dear Sir, We have no record of anything ever having gone wrong with your car." That is exactly what it means to be justified. It means that God has no record of anything ever having gone wrong in our lives.

SUBJECT INDEX

SCRIPTURE INDEX